ADVANCE PRAISE

"In *The Story in Your Head: How Life Experiences Prepare You for Leadership,* Bob Vajgrt is truly a storyteller, in what is a seamless blend of personal autobiography and professional insight. Much as in a conversation with Bob over the years, he weaves personal and professional experience into the narrative with so much ease that the listener (or reader) doesn't realize the change in the topic until one is half way though the next paragraph. The personal insight is one of a person with focus on family, and professional advice is that of a mentor. And this is who Bob is, a caring person who shares his experience with the reader. This book is a worthwhile "read" with positivity, autobiography, storytelling and a lifetime of architectural project management perspective."

—Abie Khatchadourian,
Architect and Principal, with 47 years of experience,
including several national and global architectural firms.

"Bob Vajgrt taught me one of the most important tips of my professional career: how to turn my work email off on my phone when taking paid time off. As a Type A person who struggles not being available for everyone all the time, having your **leader show you how to** *truly turn off work when you are off from work* was life changing. With this simple strategy, Bob empowered his staff to fully embrace personal time and recognized that this is imperative to not only each person's mental and physical health, but to the success of our clients, firm, and project teams. This book is full of Bob's grounded, funny, and people-focused wisdom that will benefit people at all stages of their professional and personal lives."

—Kit Dailey,
Engagement Specialist and
Principal at a national architectural firm

THE STORY IN YOUR HEAD

THE STORY IN YOUR HEAD

How Life Experiences
Prepare You for Leadership

ROBERT A. VAJGRT

The Story in Your Head: How Life Experiences Prepare You for Leadership
Published by Larger Than Life, LLC
Greenfield, Wisconsin, U.S.A.

VAJGRT, ROBERT A., Author
THE STORY IN YOUR HEAD
ROBERT A. VAJGRT

Larger Than Life, LLC
5212 South 41st Street
Greenfield, Wisconsin 53221
www.LargerThanLifeLLC.com

Library of Congress Control Number: 2025904857

ISBN: 979-8-9915549-0-9, 979-8-9915549-2-3 (paperback)
ISBN: 979-8-9915549-3-0 (hardcover)
ISBN: 979-8-9915549-1-6 (digital)
ISBN: 979-8-9915549-4-7 (audiobook)

BUSINESS & ECONOMICS / Leadership
SELF-HELP / Communication & Social Skills
BODY, MIND & SPIRIT / Inspiration & Personal Growth

Editing: Fine Lines, LLC; Lisa Shrewsberry & Madison McMillion (shrewsberry5live@gmail.com)
Cover Design: Julia Kuris (designerbility.com.au)
Book Design & E-book formatting: Amit Dey (amitdey2528@gmail.com)
Publishing Management: Susie Schaefer (FinishTheBookPublishing.com)

QUANTITY PURCHASES: Schools, companies, professional groups, clubs, and other organizations may qualify for special terms when ordering quantities of this title. For information, email info@largerthanlifellc.com

DEDICATION

To all who want to be the drop in the pond that shapes the shoreline, and to those who shaped me into who I am.

A special thanks to my wife Dawn for sharing life's adventures with me.

TABLE OF CONTENTS

Life ends, but the impact goes beyond your life.
You can affect others long after managing and leading them

FOREWORD

I define leadership as "anyone who has influence over another person." Influence comes in many ways and from everyone. The following pages are the collection of a life and career of a man that has always been a leader who influences with these core behaviors: creativity, innovation, and empathetic kindness.

There are three things that all of us have complete control over and that is our happiness, our mindset, and our engagement. Yet, we often struggle with all different types of narratives in our head. Sometimes these narratives can drive us to overconfidence. Other times they create doubt and anxiety. However, there is only one person that can challenge the stories we tell ourselves. No matter how much advice we are given, we ultimately and always have control of our choice and the direction we take.

Leading offers challenges, and our seasons of life and leadership can amplify these narratives to the point where they become so loud that our impact on others is negatively influenced because we can't focus. Leaders are, by nature, curious and reflective, as well as intentional about their influence on others.

Which is why the following pages are both a beautiful reflection and a powerful recipe. Bob's stories and life lessons are the type of wisdom that impacts us and supports our growth.

If you have the privilege in your life to meet leaders who believe that life happens for you, that obstacles are opportunities, and that every mistake is learning, well, then you are going to grow forward. Bob is that type of man.

What this book glosses over is the sheer magnitude of his influence as a leader. Bob has a demeanor that we can all learn from, a calm humbleness that is wrapped around an incredibly intelligent person, and it is found throughout this book.

As you read this text, stop and reflect after each section. Ask yourself, what have I been through that is similar and what would I have done differently if I had learned from and with Bob?

Remember, a leader leaves a piece of themselves everywhere they go, and most leaders never understand the impact they have on those around, mainly because we never see the influence in action as a result of being a role model to others. Everyone around us sees our behaviors and makes one of two decisions: 1. I will apply that tactic in my own leadership. 2. I will never do what they just did.

Bob's influence and examples in this text are important to pay attention to as he walks you through his life experiences. I can't even imagine all the ways he has impacted others. However, I can offer two quick reflections on Bob's influence on me and my family.

I was a young principal when I first met Bob, and he was lead on a project to build a new middle school in our school district. He and I worked hundreds of hours together on the design and the construction. On one particular day, Bob and I sat through and interviewed every teacher in the school about their vision and desire for the learning spaces. Now, Bob is an inspirationally innovative guy and always seeking to be cutting edge. He was attending all types of personal and professional development on innovations in classrooms and how form and design could positively impact learning.

He had shared with me a significant number of articles and videos showing all of these amazing ways that light, and furniture, as well as technology, could revolutionize the traditional spaces of learning.

However, teacher after teacher would come into the interviews and see all of this amazing stuff and respond with a strict defense of 19th century style classrooms with rows of desks all facing in one direction. Literally, after eight hours of being together, I was exhausted watching Bob give the same presentation every thirty minutes and then hearing my staff fight being innovative and demand status quo.

After the day had completed and the doors were closed, I went off with some colorful language and deep frustration because so few of the staff wanted to adopt his ideas. Bob, calm like always, completely disarmed me with the following statement: "Imagine what it would be like to be them?"

His leadership in a moment that he had every right to be frustrated and even angry was a beautiful default behavior. His default was to be empathetic, and his words caused me to be the same. His influence in that moment still impacts me because there are a lot of days when I find myself telling people all over the country the importance of suspending judgment and focusing on being empathetic.

I can't even imagine how many people Bob calmly influenced into being better leaders because of his strengths.

Now, the second story. Architects like Bob not only design structures with intent and purpose, they leave little legacies with everything they design and build. Just like leaders, architects have influence in everything from the beauty of the exterior to the intentional placement of a staircase or the reason the closets are where they are. However, they are not always brought back into the space years later to see or hear of their design's impact.

In the following pages, you will read about Bob and a project he did in Sheboygan Falls where, once again, he was leading and innovating yet running into resistance. He was working with and supporting a leader on a middle school project that was going to be disruptive to the traditional ideas or as he calls them "legacy schools." He and the superintendent demonstrated great perseverance and moved forward with an amazing design and saw it through to construction.

How does Bob's influence live on? Well, in May of 2024, a few years after the innovative project was completed, a young man graduated from St. Norbert's College with a teaching degree and was hired to work in Sheboygan Falls. When he was interviewed, they gave him a tour of the school and his future classroom. That young man left the interview and had a few others lined up; however, after he saw the school and the classroom, he wanted to work there.

That young man got the job and was insanely excited about being in this amazing space. He brought his two parents to school to see the incredible space which he was proud to be a part of and he even invited his grandparents to see the school. He utilizes the innovative design, the glass walls, the furniture package, the creative design, the collaborative spaces, and he's really proud to work in such a "cool" school.

As I write this, that young man is sitting at my kitchen table preparing his lesson for tomorrow. Bob, without even knowing it, impacted two generations of my family: me in the design of a school and my leadership, and Mr. Charlie Neitzke, my son and an 8th grade social studies teacher, at Bob's designed middle school in Sheboygan Falls.

This book will do the same for you. Read it with a highlighter, find the nuggets of a lifetime of wisdom, and change the narratives in your head. Live and lead forward with Bob's recipes for influence, strategies for your narratives, and lessons to propel you forward (propel – I had to work that in here somewhere for my friend the pilot)!

Ted Neitzke IV, CEO CESA 6,
Former Superintendent of Schools,
Principal, Teacher, Mayor of Port Washington, WI,
Author, and Host of the "Smart Thinking" Podcast

INTRODUCTION

The impact we have on others is truly larger than the life we live. We all have memories of people who made a difference in our lives through the compassion they shared, the wisdom they instilled, or the bruise left by a remark or action. All these experiences stayed with us and made us who we are today. Who you are will determine how you will manage and lead others.

As a licensed architect since 1992, I spent most of my years managing and leading others. I have worked in many market sectors including education, healthcare, retail, industrial, residential, and hospitality, each with many client topologies. I started my career in a sole proprietor firm (I was his only employee) and ended my career as a principal in a firm of over 250 employees with five offices spread across the United States.

In the middle of my architectural career, I grew hungry—not for lunch, or even for competition, but for finding ways to do things better—to be more efficient, to manage, and to lead my teams better. I wanted to be the best expert at project management I could be. I wanted to earn the title, and I wanted to absorb and retain all the important information along the way. I listened to podcasts related to my profession and attended many seminars focused on project management. I read team building books, coaching and mentoring books, leadership books, and yes—project management books.

During this time, I realized something was missing in the material I was seeking and reviewing. First, most material read like textbooks to be studied rather than "self-help" books to be applied and activated, and most who have reached the project management level are ready to put the basic education behind them and immerse themselves in the practical aspects of their discipline. Sure, there were exceptions; some had great anecdotes they used to make their point, but even these, to me, lacked the comprehensive vision of what it takes to be a great project manager.

Throughout my career, I carefully observed the good and not-so-good in people, including myself. I learned how to manage all types of clients, people, and the process of architecture itself. I took something from the vast spectrum of these experiences. My focus for more than twenty-five years, the thing I did most and ended up doing best, was Project Management Leadership, or leading clients and project teams through the entire architectural process.

With my experience leading and managing people and projects, I thought I had something to offer others to help them improve what it is they are managing, whether creating a new building or a widget. I floated the idea of writing a book about how to be a great project manager to an associate, Megan Kocchi. This was at a time when I was a principal in a firm and leading our education market. Megan was a confidant who worked with me on the marketing side of the business. She was always there to help vet my ideas, so I appreciated her honesty and advice. After leaving my career, Megan sent me a message telling me my newfound availability might allow me to author that book I always talked about. Because of Megan's message, you are reading this book and, hopefully, will gain insight on how to be a better leader and project manager.

What it takes to be a good project manager, manager of people, manager of processes, or just an overall good leader and person is determined by who you are, and who you are is predicated by your life experiences and your response to those experiences.

The life experiences you have had that impacted, shaped, and honed you into the person you are today affect how you lead and manage your team, whether your team enjoys working with you, and whether you will become a thought leader. The process of making you who you are and the ever evolving you as a project manager and leader are one in the same; we don't behave in a vacuum at home and in community and then conduct a different kind of business at work. Our job is to unify and leverage these important, ubiquitous lessons, starting with: Nothing remains the same. The shoreline is always changing.

I have often said that a project manager can manage anything. They are experts at managing, whether the managed resource is people, a process, a concept, or a client, and to lead from the front lines, always with their vision in mind. It's the person and the way they see things, their ability to predict, to anticipate, and to lead toward these predictions and anticipations that makes a great project manager. My stories and experiences will focus mainly on architecture, however, they can undoubtedly apply to any profession and are for anyone tasked with project management and leadership.

Typically, leadership is defined as setting direction or vision, influencing, motivating, and empowering others, while

Project Management is defined as controlling day-to-day tasks to meet the vision, mission, and goals of the project. To be a good project manager, you must be good at both leadership and management. I call this 3PM Leadership: Project Management Leadership, Process Management Leadership, and People Management Leadership.

Whether you prefer to keep project management and leadership distinct or, like I do, use 3PM Leadership as a more accurate descriptor, your specific approach to leadership and project management started the day you were born and has been honed, improved, (sometimes impoverished or challenged), and polished by your life and career experiences and by how you handled each element.

It is who you are—how you have allowed life's experiences to shape who you are—that will determine your success. Throughout my career, I have had the opportunity to show others who I was, the good and the not-so-good. At times, I shined brightly by being a positive and steady light for my clients and teams, while other times I shone dim and disgraced (have you ever lost your temper in front of your entire team? I have!). Here are stories, experiences, and personal accounts of how I developed 3PM Leadership, and I hope these stories resonate with you and help you consider who you are, both in life and as a project leader. My hope for you is that the experiences I share will resonate to remind you of your own life experiences that have made you who you are today, and that they will help you seek ways to improve or at least impart awareness of how you became who you are. By sharing these stories, I hope to pass on wisdom of my successes and failures as a leader, project manager, and person, and to help you feel more grounded in your own experiences and successes to more confidently manage and lead.

In February 2023, I left a thirty-five-year career in architecture. Throughout my career I managed and led people and teams. I saw a lot of people come and go from organizations looking for something that they didn't seem to have at their current job—be it money, responsibility, career advancement opportunities, bad work environment, or you name it. When people left my organization, I felt sad for us; in most cases, we were losing talent and experience. I also felt happy, though, that the people who left had decided to take a leap of faith and seek what they felt was right for them. I have often said that everyone is replaceable, which I still believe to be true. When a person vacates a position at a company a position is posted, interviews occur, and a new employee is placed into the role. Is the company the same? Will the product be the same? Will the environment be the same? The answer is no. And no doesn't mean it's better or worse, it just means it's different.

Self-esteem is how we value and perceive ourselves. This is internal to us, how we think about ourselves. However, those thoughts are affected by how others speak of us and treat us. You, yes you, can affect someone else's self-esteem. It is our job as 3PM Leaders to build others up.

Confidence is believing in yourself and your abilities; it is believing that your beliefs and abilities are right and just. This is personal and there is a level of confident visibility that, if exposed, can make you look arrogant and boastful. A good leader will have a good balance of internal and external confidence.

Leadership can be defined as leading a group of people or an organization, yet it seems like this definition is chasing its own tail. A better definition is: The ability to motivate people to achieve a common goal. Leaders motivate people to work as a team, to push the team to innovation, to mentor others so they can achieve their goals. A leader is a servant to their team, not the other way around.

CHAPTER 1

YOU, DEFINED

Who Are You?

A drop in a pond makes a small ripple that can and does affect all the water in that pond. As the ripple moves through the pond it will eventually hit a shoreline that will be changed forever. Drops can be the size of a tear or the size of cats and dogs. We all, like drops, can impact others like that forever-changed shoreline; conversely, our shorelines can be impacted by others. We can be gentle as kittens or aggressive as wild dogs. What kind of drop will you be? We have been shaped by both gentle and rough ripples—they have shaped us into who we are. What kind of drop will you be in someone else's pond? How will you affect their shoreline?

Who are you, or who do you think you are? We hear this inside of our own heads when we make a comment to someone that is out of context with our character; it's our personal accountability system activating. Like an alarm system, we should never ignore it. Danger! Danger! You are doing or saying something that is so out of character that those who know you best, your family and friends, may suddenly realize they have no idea who you are. You, yourself, may be extending beyond the boundaries of who you are. Whenever I hear that question—"Who Are You?"—my mind instantly goes to The Who, the *other* influential rock band from England, with Roger Daltrey the lead singer who sang the question verbatim. To sincerely answer this question "Who are you?" is not to give an impetuous response. I have found trying to verbalize who you are (your mission, your vision, your values, your beliefs) takes serious introspection—that is to verbalize who you say you are, not who others say you are. I am talking about the person you personify, not who you *think* you personify.

Personal accountability is something that can be learned and modeled. When you have personal accountability, it is much easier for you to hold others accountable and for others to see that you will do what you say you will do. So, the reverse is also true—you will be accountable to them as they are accountable to you. In a sense, personal accountability helps define who you are as a person.

In college, you are accountable only to you. You are responsible for your education. The professors are not responsible for ensuring that you show up to class or that you stay ahead of your homework. Your professional career is no different in that sense—you are responsible for it. To grow, nurture, and maintain yourself, you must stay ahead of things and do the necessary work—go to conferences, listen to prominent influencers in your field, see what your competition is doing and what new methods or products are available. Understanding all these perspectives and where your field of expertise is heading will allow you to leapfrog off what others are doing, or maybe even ahead of them.

We all have façades that crop up at times, and sometimes they are entirely appropriate and necessary. We sometimes show confidence when we might be a bit wobbly (fake it until you can become it). We show humor sometimes in the face of heartbreaking situations to lighten the mood for ourselves or others. We show interest when we care less but would like to care more. These façades still represent us and show who we are, however, we are presenting the image of who we want others to see and perhaps not who we truly are in thought, expression, deed, and word.

As a kid, I was probably perceived as a bit unusual. I prefer to think of it myself then as "unique" or one-of-a-kind. My mom always told me I was a trendsetter, though not from my 1970s-style clothing with wide and pointy collars, my slightly pudgy physique, or even my thick, black, military-style eyeglasses frames. Rather, she said, it was the way I took responsibility and personal accountability to the point that my sisters used to call me "St. Robert" in that I could do no wrong in the eyes of others.

A baby, it is said, develops a personality by four months after birth. By this time, they have developed their unique temperament and personality traits. These things, however, do not define one's mission, vision, values, or beliefs. These things are developed over time. Having a mission that drives you, a vision of what you want to accomplish in life, and a value and belief system that helps calibrate your moral compass are things developed and evolved over time. These, in my experience, come from relatives, friends, teachers, coworkers, grandkids, and sometimes strangers. It's true what your parents told you: We don't behave in a vacuum. You tend to become like those who surround you.

If you believe that you need redefining, it is never too late. When a person is diagnosed with cancer or has a heart attack, we often see a profound change in that person. They live life differently by cherishing every day and moment; they may be more loving and giving, and they may eat healthier and lose weight. It is never too late to redefine the person you are if you sense you need changing. Start today. Only you can change you; others may try, but only you can change yourself.

In the movie *Groundhog Day*, Bill Murray plays Phil Connors, a cynical, self-centered, egotistical weatherman sent to Punxsutawney, Pennsylvania, to cover the annual Groundhog Day festivities. Phil wakes on Groundhog Day in a bed and breakfast with Sonny and Cher's "I Got You Babe" playing on the radio. After dressing, he heads down to the dining area of the bed and breakfast and makes snide remarks to everyone he meets. He does a live shot at the Groundhog Day celebration and then quickly heads back home only to be stopped in his tracks by a snowstorm he had predicted would miss the area. Phil spends his night at the bed and breakfast he just came from waiting out the storm. When the alarm goes off in the morning, it is an exact repeat of what was on the day before— it is Groundhog Day again and again and again, until he learns each lesson the day had to offer. Changing who you are takes personal awareness that something needs to change. It takes time, but it can be done. It begins today.

Your Mission

"Your mission, should you choose to accept it," is a well-known phrase broadcast on a tape recorder from the 1966 television show *Mission Impossible*, which later became a series of blockbuster movies. Having a personal mission in life, in your career, for the project you are managing or the team you are leading, is critical to accepting it. Defining and writing down a specific mission is the first step to accomplishing it; there is power in committing a mission to words, to paper or document. It becomes embedded in your subconscious and holds you accountable. A personal mission statement guides the many micro decisions you must make to get to your destination. It is both the fuel in your gas tank and your destination—it is the thing that drives you. My personal mission statement is: "Be the person who supports and helps others accomplish their goals." This is the essence of every decision I make when it comes time to make it; it is also the definition of a servant-leader.

One shared goal between my wife and I is to travel to all parts of North America. We want to do this in a camper van. Our dream day is to arrive at a remote, serene lake's edge, park our camper van, and be completely off the grid, whiling away our remaining days soaking in our surroundings and enjoying the placidity. After stepping away from my career, my wife decided that the time was now to look for and purchase that camper van. No, this was not a spur-of-the-moment purchase during the pandemic of 2020. Ours was much more calculated and planned. When we walked into a RV showroom, we were greeted by a knowledgeable sales consultant who asked us lots of questions. To better help us, he needed more information. He wanted to understand why we wanted a camper van, what we were going to use it for, how many people would be traveling in the van, and what amenities we thought we needed… so many questions! We answered, and between my wife and I, we talked to determine what it was we truly wanted to do with the camper van. Some of the information was new to us, so we needed time to reassess. Then, our sales consultant asked, "What is your mission?" This made us stop in our tracks. Dawn and I looked at each other like deer in the headlights. This simple statement brought everything into focus. What, indeed, *was* our mission for this new adventure? The reinvigorated question helped us answer in greater detail and with improved clarity about things like the number of people we would be traveling with, the amenities we would need to be off the grid for a few days, and the types of places we wanted to go (ones that might require a tight fit!). "What is your mission?" helped us to get real with ourselves and summoned deep-seated answers to questions that were essential to achieving a successful ending.

Now, friends of ours are considering a similar purchase. They ask us questions about "HOW-E," our camper van (yes, we named our van). It's our Home On Wheels – Everywhere. Our friends are critical of some of the things our van has or doesn't have, both good and not so good. They say that our selection wouldn't work for them. I simply ask them, "What is your mission?" They, too, give me a look (similar to the look when we were asked that same question). It's funny because now, when we talk about doing something with our friends, they jokingly ask, "What's your mission?" The concept has become our mantra, of sorts, and it works!

Having a personal mission statement helps with decision making. There are compromises in life, some beneficial and some detrimental, and having a mission statement will help you decide what compromises can and cannot be made. Deciding what you will and won't accept *is everything*. Assessing which decisions are flexible and which ones are absolutes or non-negotiables is critical to keeping you moving toward your individual mission and to bringing along those you have assembled as a team toward a collective goal.

Your Vision

Prior to graduating from the Architecture program at the University of Wisconsin – Milwaukee, I had a professor who encouraged us to create a career plan. We had to look at where we were, graduating with an architectural degree, and write down the dreams and achievements we wanted to accomplish up until the day we retired. He was literally asking us to construct a roadmap to our future lives. My first thought was: "What!? This is crazy!" I didn't have any idea of what life, or my career would offer. How could I? I was in my early twenties, hadn't yet completed my degree, and here he was asking me to think about a time thirty-five years into the future?! Unless... I thought. Unless I really was constructing my future, unless that was a thing, and it was the secret—that we are co-creators of our own lives. Then, to get myself started, I reframed the assignment in terms of looking back from the end and considering what achievements, both professionally and personally, I would have accomplished by the time I retired. This tweak in mindset provided clarity and even excitement as I opened my mind to purposefully consider what the next thirty-five to forty years would look like for me.

The bookends of my career plan were graduating college and retirement—anything could happen in between. At the time of graduation, I was not yet married, although it was already planned, so that went on the list. Buying a home went on the list. Becoming a licensed architect, a partner in a firm, owning my own firm, and the like all went on the list. As this list grew, it became vital to include a timeline and an actual date for accomplishing each goal, because without a timeline (and deadlines), there is nothing holding you accountable to each steppingstone or goal. Creating a professional career plan, as I discovered, holds you accountable to you! If you didn't have this experience, this professor pushing you to plan your life, then this is your moment and now is your time. You and only you oversee your career, your life! Sure, others will help you with mentoring and passing on wisdom, although in the end it is you who must take the steps to accomplish the goals you outline for decades to come. Remember this: Your life, your career is a marathon, and you are in this for the long haul. Your goals will take time to structure and write out and much more time to accomplish. But you can't reach a destination if you haven't defined it.

Once you create the plan, make sure you look at it every once in a while and update it. You don't have to do this obsessively. Even if you tweak the plan or review it at the beginning of each year and put it away, you'll be surprised to see how much you have accomplished just having committed it to a paper or an electronic file. Add to it if you need to. Mark off the goals you accomplish (and celebrate each in your own way). Add professional updates and include personal items as well. Over time, I added things like running a marathon and becoming a pilot.

What our professor was really helping us write was a personal vision. This allowed me to begin a vision for what I wanted to accomplish in life, and it was some of the best advice I have ever received and have since passed on to many. I set out to create a career plan but ended up with a personal vision. I still have it and tweak it to this day.

Your Values and Beliefs

I grew up in a small Midwest town that was the typical 1970s social, ethnic, and racially non-diverse community. My ancestors came to America from Czechoslovakia and the Germanic areas of Europe with basically nothing. For the most part, they were self-made and successful in business through hard work and keeping family first. My grandpa, who came to America as a boy, would start a cabinetry manufacturing shop in Oshkosh, Wisconsin. He instilled in me how to be a responsible worker and make sure that I was compensated well for the good work I did.

My grandfather was one of the millions who came to the United States on a boat from Europe and passed through Ellis Island, New York, with nothing but a vision. His father didn't speak a lick of English. My grandpa started working at the age of five cleaning up at a wood mill in Oshkosh and would progress over time to establish his company building cabinets for homes and businesses. He set the example that anything can be accomplished if you put your mind to it and stick with it. I have fond memories doing things with my grandpa; he is the one who taught me how to build things and to think about how things are built. He was a foundational person for me.

I remember fondly our afternoon conversations which sometimes included my friends and cousins. He was like an oracle to me, someone who could sense things in us like how we were feeling, detecting the troubles or excitement we exuded. We would sit down and ask how we were and what we were up to. He was truly interested in what we told him; he made us—he made me—feel important. When we asked in return what he was up to, that usually changed the conversation to fishing, baking, and canning. Like him, we, too, were sincerely interested in what he was doing. This is how family traditions get passed down. I knew that if I had a conundrum, I could lay it all out for my grandpa and he would listen and provide whatever advice or council I did or didn't ask for.

What my grandpa was doing, silently and without fanfare, was building my self-esteem. He was showing interest in me, investing his time in me, making me feel good about myself. He was showing me that I had value and was also instilling values in me. Under his influence, I started working a paper route as a young teenager, as kids did back in my day. I also did chores around my house from weeding the garden, to mowing grass, shoveling snow, and sprucing up the yard. Growing up, we had to work for the things we wanted, and we saved at least part of the money we earned. In high school, I worked at a local family-owned restaurant where I started out bussing tables and advanced to lead line cook. I believe we should model and transfer a strong work ethic and money management skills into the young people for whom we are foundational.

My grandpa wasn't the only foundational person who supported my growth. My grandma was born in 1902 in Cadott, Wisconsin. Her father, my great-grandfather, had a small store in Cadott and was the first person there to own a motorized vehicle.

My grandma, while in her seventies, boarded students who were deaf and we grandkids always treated them like they were family. She taught us that even those who were not like us, related by blood, or had the same abilities deserved to be treated the way we wanted to be treated. She taught us that you must take responsibility for your actions. If you did something you knew to be wrong, you needed to fess up and make it right. Honesty was the best policy. Often, while at Grandma's, there was mischief that I, along with my sisters or cousins, got into. Grandma would matter-of-factly tell us what we did wrong and why it was wrong. She gave us immediate feedback. My grandma was modeling values and beliefs she was hoping to pass on to us, ones that we would take and make our own.

I had great examples set before me to follow and make me proud. I had these amazing, foundational people in my life, and so many others. Maybe that's what made me do it, what made me want to succeed; there were so many worthwhile and tremendous individuals who had invested in me, and I wanted to make them and others proud with what I accomplished. This can also be motivation for you: think of your foundational people, those who have invested their time and confidence in you. What values and beliefs did they or are they still modeling for you, and how will you let these examples direct your actions?

Your Morals

Morals are an individual's principles based on what is right and wrong, often conforming to societal norms in terms of acceptable behavior. Being that morals are mostly individual, there can be something in between that is still acceptable. Your sense of right and wrong is instilled from an early age and largely dependent on your upbringing and those you surround yourself with. Religion can be the basis of developing morality and can affect the individual as well as entire communities and society itself.

My hometown was walkable, and I could ride my bike pretty much anywhere around the city. My friends and I spent some days just walking around our local department store looking at the newest 45 RPM single records. On one occasion, I was by myself watching a family shop. There was a little boy, about ten years old, along with his mom, dad, and sister. The boy apparently had just had a birthday and had received money earmarked for a new skateboard. From a distance, I spied on them while they looked at all the skateboards. As happens quite often, the boy's budget was too small for the board he wanted. Sure, there were boards that fit his budget, but they were plastic and not as cool or hip as some of the others. The boy gravitated to a longer wooden board with a grip tape surface, black polyurethane wheels with concealed ball bearings, and a skid plate to protect the board when doing gnarly tricks.

Before barcodes and self-checkouts were commonplace, prices of items were stuck on the item with a price tag gun. This tag gun had a roll of stickers, and the stickers were placed on every item in a store. They were not very sticky and could be peeled off easily without damaging the item or the sticker in any way.

As I watched this family look at boards, I noticed the dad peeling the sticker off the more expensive board and replacing it with the less expensive one. What was I seeing? Here was an adult, someone I should be able to look up to, to see as a compass for right and wrong, doing something I knew was wrong. From a distance, I could also sense why he was doing it. He wanted to make his son happy, to not have him disappointed. All of this made me very uncomfortable, and I wasn't sure what to do. I thought that surely the person checking them out would notice, so I followed them to the checkout. Remember, this was a time with no self-checkout lanes. It did appear that the person at the register questioned the price, but the dad said it must have been mismarked. The family ended up walking out with the more expensive skateboard after paying an amount equal to the lesser board.

This scenario caused a moral dilemma and a mini moral crisis within me as a ten-year-old. What did I know to be right and wrong? And why hadn't right prevailed? I contemplated whether my morality was in alignment with what I had seen. Would I do something immoral to make someone or myself happy? Could I justify doing something immoral that really didn't hurt anyone? What was the harm in paying less for something? I did know it was wrong to shoplift, but what I saw didn't seem to be shoplifting.

I thought about how this was wrong. I knew that not being able to have something immediately because of lack of money was ok—it encouraged work ethic and patience in saving up for something. In turn, earning enough money to buy the thing that you wanted instilled a sense of pride. Is there a time when morality can be more fluid, more flexible to achieve something so others can be happy? This is a question that I contemplated as a child and have many times since when my moral values have been challenged. I often wonder how the dad of the family felt when he was doing what he did. What was his thought process? What internal moral struggle, or lack of morality, was occurring? I knew at the time that some people lacked morals and that such people wouldn't bat an eye to do something like switching a price tag. However, I could sense that there was a moral struggle going on with this father.

My moral compass took a spin that day but came back to true north. The event made me examine and think about what I would do in a similar situation. It made me uncomfortable; I decided I would steer clear of doing anything like it. At an early age I contemplated right and wrong. My religion and my parents helped set my morality compass. I knew if I wavered from my morality, I would have to answer to God and my parents. As a kid, I speculated that the wrath of God would dwarf the wrath of my parents.

I grew up in a neighborhood full of kids, most around my age. As kids, we did things we probably shouldn't have done. When I got home and my mom suspected some tomfoolery, she would ask something you may have heard yourself as a child. "If your friends jumped off a bridge, would you do it too?" My mom, our mothers, were instilling accountability. They were teaching us to stay true to our values, morals, and personal mission. My mom was building up my self-confidence. These moments instilled in me a desire to follow my heart and not necessarily the leader of the group.

There will be times when you go against what you believe and follow instructions like a good soldier. However, when this happens to the extreme, your personal accountability becomes dented, blemished, and compromised. I can tell you that you will carry decisions made while ignoring your morality with you for life.

Once, for instance, I was asked to put a person on a team, not just because they were well qualified and would do a great job, but because of their skin color. I am a firm believer that we should not judge by skin color. We should consider the person, who they are, and what they will bring to a team in skills, knowledge, and expertise. I did as I was told and was very uncomfortable doing so. At the time, I was not strong enough to tell my leader that I felt this was wrong and that it didn't do *anyone* a service—not the business, our team, or the individual. I failed myself by complying without voicing my opinion, which put a dent in who I was and what I stood for.

Most importantly, I failed my teammate by not standing up for them based on their merit rather than the color of their skin.

When asked to do something against your morality or belief system, consider how proceeding in that direction will affect you long term. It is often said we must pick our fights; I agree that not everything is worth fighting for. When it comes to you, however—who you are, your moral fabric—I will shout from the rooftops that these are the fights you must not back down from.

Everyone should take time to think about and document who they are within the categories of Values, Morals, and Personal Mission, as these should guide our behavior. Consider each and, just like your life or career plan, write them down.

Manage Yourself First

Before you can lead others, you must first understand who you are.

Stress has both good and bad effects on the human body. Good stress can be like an adrenaline rush, helping you stay laser-focused, boosting energy, and heightening awareness. However, bad stress can be debilitating. Bad stress is when pressure is applied from multiple directions with unacceptable consequences. You're given a work assignment that interferes with vacation. Or you have personal responsibilities you are not getting done because work responsibilities keep stacking up against them. You must have an awareness of both good and bad stress and not let bad stress get too far entrenched in your soul. I am certain—and research proves—that stress, over time, can affect the body in negative ways. What's worse, or cumulative, is that too much stress makes you miss the big picture; it eats away at your vision.

I had left a firm to seek greener pastures; actually, I was looking for more opportunity. I found out that the other pasture is not always greener.

My wife and I were months away from having our first baby when I joined my new firm. Bringing a new life into the world is a life-changing event that requires time to establish a family bond and experience a flood of emotions that words cannot describe. When a child, especially the first, is born, there is such a sense of awe and unconditional love that it is overpowering. It exceeds the Richter scale. I wanted to be a part of creating a parental bond with my wife and the new life we created, so I had planned on taking all my vacation, a full two weeks, at once.

When I joined the firm, I told my new employer of my impending arrival and that I was going to take my two weeks of vacation to spend time with my wife and new baby to bond together as a family. I got the standard, supportive answer: "Of course! Take the time to be with your family."

Our son was born on a Thursday in June. He was the first baby I ever held, so I handled him like a fragile piece of glass. When we got him home, my wife and I looked at him in wonder as we laid him in his cradle. Then, we looked at each other and wondered what we should do with him next. He just stared back at us; I think he was wondering what to do next, too. And so began our adventure to create a family by spending the next two weeks focused solely on each other.

To my surprise and heartbreaking disappointment, my project manager called me only a few days into the following week. He wasn't calling to see how we were doing; sure, he asked, but the real reason came next: "So, when are you coming back to work?" I was in shock. I had been gone for only four days! I wasn't coming back for another week, and we had all agreed on that, or so I thought. He explained that there was a lot of work that needed to be done, and they needed me. I acquiesced and we compromised that I would come in half a day for the duration of my time off. After all, I was new to the company and didn't want to jeopardize my employment. Every time I think of this, I think about my lack of confidence, my lack of standing by my values and beliefs.

This showed me that the firm didn't really care about its employees and their wellbeing. I thought to myself that if I ever grew to attain a position of leadership, I would hold true to what I said regardless of the sacrifice needed to help my teammates.

While at the same company, I became a leader on the architectural side of the business. As in any company, there was turnover of staff. However, turnover can provide opportunity, and that opportunity can lead to moving up the corporate ladder. As team members left, I moved closer to the top of the organization and into a higher leadership position. I discovered that the closer to the top of an organization you get, the hotter the flame.

Leaders, I thought at the time, should spend time with their teams and help where they can regardless of the task, even sweeping the floor if necessary. They need to put in more time than their teammates, and that is what I did, but it was at a great cost. I pitted my work life against my personal life. This led to an almost unbearable amount of bad stress. I had on the schedule for a month to take a four-day weekend camping trip with my family; I would take a Thursday and Friday off to expand the weekend. It wasn't a full vacation, but I had already worked over forty hours that week before taking the time my family needed.

When the president of the company found out that I was taking a four-day weekend, I was called into his office. The president informed me, in a rather coarse and voluminous way, that taking four days off meant the firm would not have revenue coming in and that I needed to rethink my vacation. The firm needed me to have billable time on projects. I calmly explained to him that I had planned this time off; it was on the calendar and my work was stable to a point that I was able to leave it for a few days. Again, this time with a raised voice and stern tone, the president stated that my time off meant no revenue was being produced and I could not take off.

I don't recall exactly what I did about the vacation, however, it was only three long months after this discussion that I left the firm. This added to the amount of bad stress that had been building over time.

Aside from the mounds of medical data proving that stress is a silent killer, I know from experience. During my time at this firm, I was diagnosed with cancer and another temporary paralyzing condition that could only be explained as my body's response to insurmountable stress. A person's wellbeing is more important than any paycheck. I learned so I could pass along to you now to take care of yourself and your family first; it is a decision you will never regret.

People will take what you give to them; you must hold true to who you are. You are special, you are one of a kind with your own values and morals; hold tight to them and don't allow them to be skewed. Will you be able to sleep at night if you deviate? I hope not. Don't ask someone else to do something that you yourself are not prepared to do. Don't deliver a message that does not feel right or mesh with who you are and what you believe. Don't fold under the pressure. You'll know the times I'm referring to, when it's better to just walk away.

Have courage to leave the pack and head in a different direction. Take the path less traveled or not traveled at all, the one that makes most sense to you. You'll be amazed at what you find and the freedom you experience!

This is exceedingly difficult to execute. We hear it all the time in the workplace and the world in general. How many times have we heard people say they are fed up with their job, yet they keep coming back day after day? Even in our society, we often hear people say that when the opposing political party wins the presidency, they will leave the country. But do you know anyone who has done this? People don't always do what they say, especially when disgruntled.

Everything changes; nothing—and I mean nothing—stays the same. People change over time, corporations change, and so does our way of thinking. Even though change is inevitable and can be very good, not all change will fit into your beliefs and morals. When this happens, a personal struggle ensues. How will you manage your reaction? I have had several of these examples presented to me over my life and have dealt with them head-on using my beliefs, values, and morals as guideposts.

Like with many licensed professions, becoming an architect requires the successful completion of multiple exams and years of experience. While working for a mid-sized firm for about three years, I successfully took and passed the required tests to become a licensed architect. I filled out the paperwork, sent it in along with recommendation letters, and in a few months received my architectural license in the mail from the State of

Wisconsin. I was officially an architect—I even had a stamp that said so. It was an achievement that I was very proud of. In school we were told that only forty-five percent of those who took the exams were successful, which made me feel especially good about myself and my achievement.

Once I had my license, I thought it was time to ask for more opportunity. This was the first time in my career I was going to ask for something, and I was a bit nervous. The words that my grandpa often said popped into my head: "The worst thing anyone can say is no." With those words of wisdom, I was prepared for anything. I approached one of the owners of the firm with my wonderful news and asked how my role in the firm might change or progress; he stated it would stay the same and gave me a dismissive glance. Talk about deflating a balloon! I thought because I was a licensed architect, I could bring more value to the firm. I could take on more responsibility and tasks. I also thought that a raise was in order. The partner's response left me with a feeling that the firm had no interest in having me take on more leadership or doing any of the other things that a young, aspiring architect wanted. I got the worst answer—"No."

I really liked the people I was working with and the firm itself. It was a good and well-respected firm, but if opportunity to fulfill my career plan were not present there, I felt I needed to start looking for other opportunities. The "no" had pushed me to an affirming "yes," spoken to myself; I was valuable, and my career was important. So, I started to seek out other firms.

This same independent thinking forced me to change mortgage companies when the one we had was changing the terms of our loan due to it being bought out. After days of phone calls and trying to work with them, I told them I would be paying the mortgage in full and going to another firm. I was certain that the mortgage banker thought I was bluffing. Like the Kenny Rogers song says, "You got to know when to hold 'em, know when to fold 'em." Bluffing might work in cards, but it rarely works out in real life situations. When you say something, be prepared to follow through no matter how difficult the road ahead may seem or how high the mountain may be to climb.

My wife and I worked diligently with a mortgage broker we trusted and valued and within weeks, we were banking with a new mortgage company. When you do things like this, make a change, take a step, look up to the presumably unattainable, and follow through with what you say, you will be surprised at the peaks you will peer down from and the green grass you will walk into.

Don't be afraid or over-egoic to think that you can hang on to anything—a job, a project, a client, or a mortgage company—when things go astray. If things aren't working, bail. You're not a tree; if you don't like where you are, move. Hand the project off to another project manager who might have more success building the client relationship or connecting better. I'm not saying to doubt yourself but be honest with yourself and manage your own reality first; don't fool yourself into toughing it out when you're forcing a fit. That's dangerous territory for yourself and for others, and it is nothing but ego. It is okay to allow a different project manager to take the conversation to a level that you could not, if you realize this is what needs to happen. It's ok to walk away from a project or a client. Think of it as allowing others to succeed where you would have had less success. Also, if you are spending time on a project you don't belong on, what is happening with the project where you do belong? You wouldn't want anyone else—someone not as qualified or as enthusiastic and capable—to step in where you were meant to be. Isn't recognizing this a sign of true success and leadership? I believe that it is.

When I became studio director, I challenged my team to BOOGIE. It was something that I picked up from a conference I had attended. "BOOGIE" – Be Outstanding Or Get Involved Elsewhere—was something that I always kept tucked away in my brain. It was freeing. I tucked it away and saved it for times I thought I might not be giving my best or getting the best. It was this word, this concept, that in the late winter of 2023 caused me to recognize that I wasn't outstanding and wasn't providing outstanding service to my team or clients, so I BOOGIED and decided to get involved elsewhere. I took a risk and left my firm and my profession to seek out where I could BOOGIE once again.

CHAPTER 2

MAINTAINING A CREATIVE MINDSET

Be Open to the Unknown

Close your eyes and think back to your elementary school days. My elementary school was typical of the times with a large cafeteria, gymnasium, and a corridor lined on each side with classrooms organized by grade level. If your school was like mine, it was a potpourri of smells—crayons, cleaning agents, cafeteria foods. Who didn't love taking a moist blue mimeograph copy and slowly raising up to take a deep refreshing breath of an assignment born? I'm sure I killed a few brain cells doing that; it was one of those sensory experiences you will always remember. Whether that was before your time or not, now think back to your art room. It was, for me, one of my favorite rooms to spend time in. There were so many interesting things in the art room to mesmerize an elementary kid. There was an endless array of colored paper and containers full of supplies like paint brushes, tools for clay, markers, and crayons; lining the walls were works of art bursting with shape, texture, smell, and color. It was an explosion for the senses!

Art class really had no rules; we could create anything. My favorite time was when we got to work with clay. We could create whatever our little minds could imagine. Although I do recall an abundance of clay ashtrays being made for Christmas gifts, most generations can relate to the piles of brown or gray clay we were to knead into the wonders which lay vividly in our minds. Oh, there was *one* important rule we had to follow—keep the clay thin to eliminate air bubbles. An air bubble in your sculpture could spell doom for your masterpiece and those around it as it got heated to the temperature of the sun in a kiln. Air bubbles can get super-heated to the point of explosion, sending the clay shrapnel of your creation into your classmate's work of art. Firing of clay, from our art room, usually happened over the weekend, so on Monday it was always a sense of victory (or possibly agony) when you walked into the art room to identify your sculpture and see if it had survived the firing.

Art class allowed us to get messy, to create without boundaries, to think beyond reality, to see beauty in a way that others could not recognize. This was true freedom, being expressive with visual arts through thought and creation. No one asked to see an example of what you were creating because it didn't yet exist—it was supposed to be one of a kind. Having that kind of flexibility and freedom to think beyond what is known, to create something that no one has seen before, is true innovation and creativity in action.

Like art class, project management involves getting messy and solving problems, most of which will require a solution that has to be invented. It's coming up with a solution that goes beyond the known. Sometimes, coming up with innovation is messy and, yes, can sometimes lead to your creation blowing up in the process and taking others out at the same time. Even though the process of what we do is repetitive, the project is different every time, and we can't be afraid to do what has never been done before. That is the very definition of innovation.

I managed school projects for more than twenty-five years and worked with many public-school districts and private schools. Each project involved a process that included pre-design, schematic design, design development, construction documentation, and finally, construction. The same process was used on every project, but the design and the solution to address the client's mission, needs, and priorities was different every time. Developing unique, individualized solutions requires creativity that is open to new ideas, and it may need to be completely innovative—something that has not been done before, something unknown.

We often hear, "Don't reinvent the wheel," and I understand the point, however this can stub creativity. When I hear this adage, I tend to think, is there something better than a wheel that isn't a wheel? Maybe the wheel isn't the best design. How do we get to the next thing if we can't get beyond thinking what we have is already the best thing? Maybe we should think more like an elementary-age child so our minds can go beyond what we know, becoming open to the unknown.

While working with the Sheboygan Falls School District (SFSD), a district located in central eastern Wisconsin, just miles from Lake Michigan, I understood their goal was to create a new school that departed from schools of the past. I like to call schools of the past "legacy schools." Legacy schools are those which we see when looking at the definition of "school" in Webster's Dictionary, the kind of school I described above and that many of us attended. SFSD wanted spaces that would support students and teachers in all modalities of learning and teaching and be flexible to changing pedagogies over time. Understand that sometimes getting to this point of departure from the ordinary takes time because change is uncomfortable.

This project stalled for quite some time while the district worked through many possible solutions, finding one that the community would support. During the entire process, we challenged staff to think differently, to change their mindsets as to what school meant, how it was organized, and what designs would best support students and teachers. We had many sessions with staff where we would review design options and take feedback.

During one design meeting, staff kept coming back to a design they knew—one they were comfortable with, one that was not unique nor met the vision they had set. Jean Born, the Superintendent of Schools, and I sat solemnly in the conference room after everyone left. Jean raised her head and looked at me with an expression of defeat, asking what I thought of the staff's solution. I recognized this as one of those moments when expertise and leadership in your field must shine brightly. It was also a time when giving your professional opinion could bruise a few egos, but your honest advice must still be given. I took a moment and thought, "If I don't stand up and lead this district through this process of creating a unique solution, they will miss out on their mission and vision." I looked at Jean and told her that the staff's thoughts were based on what they knew, what they were comfortable with, and that this was not going to meet the mission nor vision they had set out to accomplish. They were creating a legacy school that would no longer meet the needs of the students and teachers. Jean was relieved that I recognized what she also saw. She told me that we were not going to create a legacy school and that we would follow the mission and vision the team had created; she would lead the group through a change they weren't comfortable with or ready for. Working with the SFSD's Visionary Team, we again worked through a series of guiding principles which directly supported innovation. One principle centered around the community and the history that comes with it.

The Sheboygan River winds through the rolling contours of the City of Sheboygan Falls and remains a historic lifeforce of the community for industry, agriculture, and gathering. The concept of the "river" as center became a unifying principle for this project; it was a concept the staff started to get excited about. This was the drop of openness that led those involved to include a flood of many innovative ideas.

The river concept supported the innovation to create a space that would connect all activities in the building and serve as a gathering place for learning, socialization, small and large group activities, and lunch. The legacy of a large lunchroom for hundreds of students was abandoned and reimagined as lunch happening along the "river" in multiple areas of the building. This space could then also be used for students during the school day as breakout spaces. The openness to creating a space—a place staff had not seen before—led to many other innovative design solutions within the unifying theme, such as opportunities to disperse functions like art, culinary arts, Project Lead the Way (PLTW), and dedicated student service space throughout the building along the river. The river space is often utilized for student activities, staff breakout areas, and lunch.

Through the leadership of Jean, who helped staff cope with the idea of change by truly listening and encouraging mutual understanding, true innovation came to life. Change is messy and can be debilitating and scary, but it is inevitable. The change we were able to navigate through will have a positive, lasting effect for students and teachers for generations to come.

Seek First to Understand is one of the *Seven Habits* outlined by educator, author, businessman, and motivational speaker Steven Covey. I believe he uncovered a universal truth—to be a creative problem- solver, you must first seek to understand. The same applies to project management. You must answer the questions: What is the client trying to solve? What issue(s) do they want to address? Most people hear the beginning of the conversation outlining the problem and immediately start thinking of how to solve the problem. Unfortunately, they have not heard the entire problem, and therefore they have not understood what the client is looking for. Anyone who has ever interviewed anyone knows that the first things discussed are generally small talk, getting-to-know-you and settling in kinds of things. It's the same reason the character Columbo always said, "Just one more thing…"—oftentimes, the essential things are saved until last. To truly understand a client takes clarification, investigation, and excellent listening skills to develop a focus and eliminate ambiguity. Only then can you solve the problem.

When a problem is identified, we tend to retreat to our memory Rolodex and start looking for a solution we or someone else has used before that might fit. We have perceived, and now we're trying to associate with what is known. This, however, is not innovation. This may give you a good start or reference point to solving a problem, however, that solution you or someone else used once before may limit your thought processes and create a closed mind. Be open to a new way of thinking, and don't be afraid to invent something new. Now you may be thinking, "Sounds like we may be reinventing the wheel here!" You may be right, however, if you start and stay with the wheel, you may never actually come up with a unique solution.

Michelangelo, the Italian born Renaissance sculptor, painter, architect, and poet was the perfect creative mind. His life was devoted to innovation and creativity. He contemplated all aspects of life from how the human body worked, to the mystery of flight, to mastering art and mechanical engineering. All these contemplations helped make him better at each of his creative endeavors.

I believe a truly creative person can see and innovate in ways others cannot. I also believe that, with patience, focus, and determination, anyone can be a creative. Creativity comes in many forms. Some people are visually artistic, while others are musicians or composers, and still others write or, like me, create within a space. Having a creative mind in a creative profession such as architecture is vital. However, having exposure to many creative outlets allows for deep, rich connection to the ethereal world with application in the real world.

Clients often tell us that they want their building design to be ahead of the trend. To be what is next, not what has been. How do you stay ahead of trends or think of what is next? You must be open-minded, knowing that you don't know what's next or you haven't seen it before. We are talking about innovation.

As an architect, one of my biggest challenges is to help people think differently about the problem they want to solve. Open-mindedness is essential when trying to provide innovative solutions, and often I am opening people's minds to unfamiliar and new possibilities to help change their mindset.

When a client says they want something innovative, they are asking for something new, something they haven't seen, something that hasn't been done before. Quite often, when presenting a new, innovative idea, I am asked by a client to show them where it has been done before. How can something be innovative if it's already been done?

Think about the rapid pace of change since the turn of the 21st century. We communicate and exchange information differently: FaceTime, YouTube, Facebook, Snapchat, Instagram, and on and on. We get our news differently: through instant messaging and texts, streaming sources, X (née Twitter), Reuters, Digg, Google News, and on and on. Think about how we travel around our communities: Uber, Zipcar, Segway, scooters, bike rental stations, etc.

All these changes required people to think differently, to change their mindsets. But how do we do that? How do we get others to change their mindsets so they can think differently, too? When change is proposed, we often hear one of these typical responses: "We've always done it this way"; "That was good enough for me"; "Why do we have to change?" Therein lies the problem: how do we get others to give up what they know, what they perceive as the only way or perhaps the best way of doing something? I offer the following three ideas to help you think differently, to move toward having a more creative mindset.

1. Unlock Your Imagination

Once you unlock your imagination you can start to think radically different from what you know. This allows you to problem-solve in a fantasy world that eventually can become reality. Case in point, some of today's technological advances can be attributed to the TV series *Star Trek*. What was first merely imagination has now become reality, like my handheld communicator... although I am still waiting on the transporter. If it can be imagined, it can eventually become reality.

Gene Roddenberry's *Star Trek* was full of imaginative and futuristic gadgets, some of which became reality and are utilized today. Everyone on the Starship Enterprise had a personal communicator that could be flipped open to hail other crew members practically anywhere in space. Today, we have a similar device we call a cell phone. There was the universal translator that helped the crew communicate with other planetary indigenous people. Today, our phone has a translator built right into it that works in the same way, allowing us to communicate in languages we do not speak.

The transporter was used in almost every episode of *Star Trek* to dematerialize the human body and rematerialize it at another location. "Beam me up, Scotty," is an iconic phrase associated with the transporter that has yet to be invented, but I believe that if you can conceive it, someday it will come true.

When I worked in an architectural firm, I created what I coined as "Imagucation Day." This was a day where our entire Learning Environments team would think differently about what school looked like. We were innovative in our thinking and explored unique and imaginative solutions to school; we would reimagine education. We started our Imagucation Day with an exercise that would open our minds to think differently, which often involved a team exercise of solving an "impossible problem." Build a bridge with spaghetti and marshmallows; build a tower with toothpicks and paper clips; build the tallest structure possible with balloons. These problem-solving games, which might resemble something you did in middle school or high school math class, became fertile ground for the imagination of adults when applied to project management. They were a way for us to practice opening our minds to different possibilities. It allowed us to become malleable as we delved into reimagining learning environments. At the end of Imagucation Day, we had brainstormed imaginative tools, ideas, and concepts that we could start to employ immediately while others would need to wait until we developed the technologies to accomplish the task. These days allowed us to let go of what we knew to be true.

Unlocking your imagination is like doing stretching exercises with your brain. Prior to going for a run, I stretch my muscles to get them ready. Doing stretching exercises for your brain like what I described above will help you unlock potential. There are many activities such as mind puzzles, meditation, and physical exercise which can lead to opening your imagination. Stretching your imagination past the brink of reality is when true innovation happens. Perhaps the transporter went too far, however you must stretch past the absurd to get to true innovation.

2. Let Go of What You Know to be True

By asking "what if" statements, you begin to let go of what you know to be true. What if we didn't have a rotary dial on our phone and what if we didn't need a wire to connect things? These questions have led to true innovation. Someone first had to ask them. Letting go of what we know helps open the mind to think differently about problems and solutions.

Western Electric asked a question in 1941: was there a way to replace a rotary dial with numbered push buttons on a telephone? The system was developed and tested, but due to the technology limitations at the time, it was unreliable and therefore shelved until the invention of the transistor. Over the next forty years, phone companies would ask, "What if?" of this technology, and it developed to a point where rotary phone technology became obsolete and touch-tone systems ruled. The companies that advanced phone technology let go of what they knew to be true in rotary phones to develop a new touch-tone phone technology. Apple picked up the "What if?" and has advanced phone technology to indispensable touch screens. I wonder—what's next for the handheld communicator?

Today we take Bluetooth technology for granted. I get frustrated when I must physically connect two devices together with a wire! Growing up in the 1970s, we played and listened to music on vinyl records, tape cassettes, and 8-track tapes. Sure, we had portable transistor radios we could walk around with, and we could even connect a headset to them for private listening. However, that headset had a wire that was plugged into the radio. In 1979, Sony introduced the

Walkman, which allowed people to walk around with a small tape cassette player and a plugged-in headset. Today, fifty years later, we listen to music from our electronic devices with wireless ear bud technology. Someone had to ask the question, "What if we didn't have to connect a wire to our headsets?" What once seemed unimaginable is now a way of life.

Questioning gives rise to potential creative solutions. One question we must ask when challenging what we know to be true is: "Why is it that way?" Every great innovation started with a question, whether spoken or thought. And the root of the question was letting go of what we knew to be true.

3. Listen (So You Can Reflect)

Thinking differently requires us to listen to the perspectives of others. To hear other perspectives, we need to expose ourselves to them and truly listen, then we must take time to reflect on those differing views.

One of the most successful stories of changing a mindset was the 1970 *Apollo 13* mission. It's an example of listening to others, absorbing what they are saying, and then changing a mindset to accomplish a goal. As uttered in the *Apollo 13* movie: "Failure is not an option." It is a statement that changed the mindset from impossible to possible.

Three men were traveling through space destined to reach the moon, when days into the mission an explosion changed their moon landing goal. Fifty-six hours into the mission, while on a trajectory to the moon, the spacecraft had a catastrophic explosion in the service module which housed the propulsion and life support systems. The spacecraft Jim Lovell, John Swigert, and Fred Haise occupied was irreparably damaged. In addition to the service module, the spacecraft also consisted of a command module, nicknamed the *Odyssey*, and a lunar lander, nicknamed *Aquarius*. The explosion had punctured oxygen tanks that were supplying life-giving oxygen to the astronauts.

At mission control, engineers for the mission and companies that built the spacecraft gathered to problem-solve the successful return of the three astronauts. The mission had changed; this was no longer a landing on the moon mission, but a mission to bring the astronauts home alive. The team had to listen to all the information available, the varying points of view, and then they could come up with a well thought out solution to successfully bring the astronauts back to earth.

Having three people in *Aquarius* meant cramped quarters and, as time went on, a buildup of carbon dioxide as the filters weren't designed to accommodate three astronauts. There were spare filters aboard the command module and the lunar module that scrubbed the carbon dioxide from the air, however they were different shapes and therefore not interchangeable.

Mission control and the crew had to figure out a way to take a filter from the command module and fit it into the lunar module, essentially fitting a square peg into a round hole. This required creative thinking and listening to ideas while using only the resources available on board the two spacecraft. Eventually, they had a "homemade" air filtration system. Getting to this point required a mindset of

"I'm possible" over impossible. Even though it seemed impossible at the time, not coming up with a solution was not an option. Everyone had to throw the book of everything they knew away and write a new one. They had to set their prejudices aside, listen to others' opinions and ideas, take time to reflect on those ideas, and then act.

When looking to do something different, to create a better experience and to be innovative, remember to unlock your imagination by stretching your brain and letting go of what you know to be true, then listen and reflect. By being flexible and teachable in this way, anything is possible. Beam me up, Scotty!

Get Messy

When I stepped away from my profession to retire early, I was nervous, scared, and even considered what I was doing to be shortsighted. I had a great career at a great firm, I was a principal and shareholder of my firm, and I was making a comfortable salary. What was I doing?!

The whole purpose of stepping away was to have time to think about what was next for me. Let's face it, when working more than forty hours a week, doing volunteer work, taking care of one's own parents, staying connected to my adult children (who never stop needing their parents), there is little time for deep thought. So, as I was preparing to step away, I thought a personal retreat would be a good way to recenter myself and sort out my thoughts. I searched the web for personal retreats focusing on change or transitions—something that would help me reflect on what might be next for me.

The retreat I found was entitled "Transitions and New Beginnings" and was several hours away from home, situated in a turn-of-the-20th-century monastery. The retreat promised rest and renewal while reflecting on life's journey: past, present and future. This sounded like exactly what I needed!

The retreat was facilitated by Sandy Salvo with Centered Connections and Barb Bickford with Bickford Collaboration. Both Sandy and Barb are skilled at facilitating collaborative and meditative group sessions. The retreat kicked off Friday evening with a meal and welcoming session in a candlelit room where we would introduce ourselves and share the reason we were at this retreat. Our first full day of the retreat dove deeper into our transition or new beginning. My identified transition was moving from one thing to the next, or moving from a career to something else, if there was a something else. Others in the group were transitioning past the loss of a loved one, and I'm sure there were many other worthwhile reasons attendees sought out the retreat. The facilitators talked about our new beginning or transition as a threshold and asked us to consider what thresholds we needed to cross to have a new beginning. We each identified some of the things holding us back from making a new beginning or transition. I identified my thresholds, the things holding me back, as stability within my current career, being financially stable, having much knowledge about and being considered a thought leader in my field of expertise. These were all things that made me feel secure, and it was going to be hard to leave that security behind. These were the thresholds I needed to cross to be able to create a new beginning and transition from my current career to something else.

Once we had time to identify and reflect on our thresholds, we were instructed to select a "Climer Card" that visually related to our thoughts. A "Climer Card" is a tool to spark creativity, enhance dialogue, and foster deeper connections.

Through their imagery, Climer Cards are meant to inspire storytelling and metaphorical thinking (www.climercards.com).

The Climer Card I selected had an image of stacked rocks, which for a hiker on a trail is called a cairn. This seemed to best fit my thoughts of having the ability to be stable while balancing life's heavy things such as finances, career, happiness, and personal fulfillment. We were then to take this image and create an intuitive painting that was intended to help us express our emotions within color, texture, and form. WHAT?! Paint in front of people? Now, I consider myself a decent artist, but painting in front of strangers made me a bit uncomfortable. I am here to calm myself and open my mind to new ideas, I told myself, so I took a cleansing breath, grabbed a few tubes of acrylic paint and a few brushes, and I started to paint.

We were painting not a landscape, portrait, or still life but an abstract representation of our feelings. Being somewhat artistic, I immediately thought of painting something recognizable. My wife and family often tell me that I am a perfectionist. I like things to be just right, and I strive for perfection in everything I do. This new thought of creating a painting of my emotions, something that didn't have a road map or preconceived conclusion, was outside my comfort zone. I was apprehensive to start a painting I had no plan for. I was afraid of failure, of losing my ideals of the perfect painting, and of losing some of my identity.

Barb told us it was ok for the painting to be messy. The idea of being messy resonated with me and allowed me to make a mess and be ok with it. I kept saying to myself, "It's ok to make a mess. It doesn't need to be perfect." What I discovered was that I could just let myself be free to express emotion and feeling without any expectations of perfection. I started mixing colors and painting heavy objects that represented the heavy things I was feeling and thinking about and looking to bring balance to. I tried to paint all my feelings, the ones that were weighing me down, those that brought joy and light-heartedness and ones that helped bind everything together. My finished painting would not hang in an art museum, but I do have it in my office as a daily reminder that it is ok to get messy, to set out on a journey without a destination in mind and still have a successful outcome.

Life can sometimes get messy and that's ok. Mess teaches us that we can make a mess, consider why the mess happened, and then take steps to clean up the mess (if the mess is a mess that needs cleaning up). You've heard the phrase "happy accident" coined by Bob Ross, and this is true. Sometimes we have messes that improve the quality of something, and we learn from these messes, which helps us grow. I've taken that attitude from the retreat and started doing things that I knew would be messy. I've realized that when I don't allow myself to get messy, I limit my potential and my creativity. It's only paint and canvas. It's easier to say than to execute, but I can paint over the mess; I can get a new canvas.

I have applied "getting messy" to my life and I try to get messy when I feel I am sinking into the quicksand of comfort. I believe getting messy opens more options, extends possibilities, and allows you to take chances and make mistakes. Mistake is too strong a word; maybe it's just a blemish on a painting. After all, all you must do is wait for the paint to dry and then, if it truly isn't what you wanted, you can paint a brand new you right over the old one or even work the mistake into the masterpiece.

It Is as It Is Supposed to Be

How do you see a sign that is being put in your path, a sign that God may have placed there and wants you to follow? I believe we often ignore signs or are completely oblivious to them. There are opportunities for us to make a difference in lives tangent to us when these signs are placed before us. Being open, having a "Jedi" sense as to when things happen and recognizing the potential can make a ripple in the universe. It's a larger-than-life moment.

There are people who will be present in your life in passing, perhaps for only a few minutes, and others you will have for most of your life. Have you ever wondered who you would be or what your life would look like if some of these people hadn't affected you in some way?

In the classic movie, *It's a Wonderful Life*, George Bailey, played by the great actor and WWII pilot Jimmy Stewart, spent a lifetime in Bedford Falls, helping others at the sacrifice of his own needs and goals. The story finds George in dire straits. Standing at the railing of a bridge on a snowy winter's evening overlooking a river, George contemplates ending it all by jumping into the icy cold river below. Seconds from jumping in to commit suicide, someone else jumps. Now, George jumps in to save someone else from doing the same. George was saved from his life-ending intention by his guardian angel, Clarence, who knew that if he jumped in the river, George would jump in to save him. George finds himself in a bridge house drying off his wet clothes, talking with Clarence. While still feeling hopeless, George tells Clarence he wishes he had never been born. And—poof—just like that, Clarence makes it so that George had never been born. We watch as George goes back to town looking for his wife and kids. Only everything had changed, from the name of his hometown to people he never knew he had affected positively, to having no wife and therefore none of his precious children. There are more alarming things because George was never born, just as there would be if you were never born. We all leave impressions, large and minute; we are connected, sometimes long-term, sometimes short-term, but we can't imagine how life would be if those encounters never happened!

Jerry Bruscato, a former co-worker of mine, was one of the people I knew who had a positive lasting impact on me and many, many others. First impressions of Jerry could be that he was arrogant, forceful, and uncaring. Jerry was the type who would often, under his breath, lob a sarcastic remark your way about something you were not doing correctly. He danced on the line between offensiveness and delight. Jerry was a principal of the firm and at times led a market of twenty-five-plus staff, as well as the firm's principal-in-charge of firm-wide production standards, which meant he had a bit of influence. Once you got to know Jerry, you could see that his harshness was a way for him to help others be more open in thought, to consider other perspectives and solutions.

There was a major mall redevelopment project the firm was involved in that had dozens of buildings either being constructed or renovated. This project required multiple project teams and managers and, since my workload was light, I was assigned to assist Jerry. This was a very complex project, as it involved retail buildings being constructed without a known occupant or tenant. The developer was working on getting tenants for the buildings, and as tenants were identified, sometimes the building needed to change to accommodate their specific needs. One building had to be redesigned to hold a swimming pool on the second floor! Over several years, buildings were designed, redesigned, and then redesigned again, with some changes occurring while the building was already under construction or had been constructed!

One instance during a morning construction meeting, the owner asked what was being done on a particular building at the very moment the steel skeleton of the building was being erected. The owner told the contractor to call out to the field and tell them to set down whatever steel was in the air and to stop work. We all were flabbergasted and sat there for a second contemplating the ramifications. The owner indicated that a new tenant had different requirements for the building and the structure, including the concrete foundations that were already cast into the earth. The entire building would need to be redesigned! We spent the next few days reviewing the new requirements and assessing if and how we could reuse and modify the material already on site to fit into the owner's new requirements.

The life of a project for an architectural team is first conceiving an idea, creating documentation over months, possibly years, so that a contractor can then construct this never-before-seen building. There is a lot of time, emotion, and passion put into each project, as well as a sense of maternal pride that comes with birthing a set of documents and then watching the building rise from the earth. When a change is made or a new design is requested, there is the potential for resentment to occur. The resentment can tip over into anger and spitefulness, and controlling this resentment is critical for a project team's morale.

When this project was put on hold and a redesign was dictated, resentment was palpable within our team. Jerry very calmly pulled the project team together and, with a soothing tone, reframed the situation as an opportunity to give the client what they wanted. He also presented the redesign as an opportunity to do another project, reminding us we would get paid for our rework, which was just like having a new project come in the door.

Abrupt though he may have been at times, Jerry led a new narrative, causing us to react positively rather than negatively. Jerry showed me that looking for the positive can immediately help turn the tide of opinion within a project team toward the better. If Jerry had not been on the team, this may not have happened, jeopardizing the entire client-team relationship. The presence of mind Jerry imparted had a lasting impact on me. Jerry's effect on others can be imagined just like George Bailey's. Jerry has since passed, but I think about the lasting impressions he left with me quite often. Thanks, Jerry.

Go Where None Have Gone Before

I recently read the book *The Wright Brothers* by David McCullough. The story of the Wright brothers, Orville and Wilbur, is about taking chances and doing something no one else has done before. Orville and Wilbur sought to create a machine flown by a person, which was different than just creating a flying machine. While they looked at what others were doing at the time, their innovation was an entirely new concept; they literally wrote the book on how to fly an aeroplane. They set goals, created guiding principles, and worked to achieve them while not having previous examples to fall back on. That's true innovation!

The Monona Grove School District is made up of two cities, Monona and Cottage Grove, both located around the

Madison, Wisconsin area. The district selected a few teachers from all their elementary schools to be on a visionary team, which would work through the process of determining how a new 3rd through 5th grade school would serve students and staff. The team created five guiding principles, one of which would directly impact how they thought about space and its use.

The new school was to unite Monona and Cottage Grove by providing spaces and services accessible to all students, staff, and community members. Spaces would be designed to promote collaboration and foster relationships. Like the project previously referenced in Sheboygan Falls School District, we would not be designing another legacy school; we would be innovators. It was time to get messy.

As we worked through programming spaces for the new school, the visionary team talked about the cafeteria and how they wanted it to be more of a dining room table feel rather than a dining hall feel. They wanted to create a space where teachers could sit with the students at lunch time and chat, rather than having a large cafeteria where 300 students would gather for lunch. With that thought, our design team brought up the idea of creating small cafés to serve 100 students within each grade wing. We talked about the space being available to the grade wing during the school day as a makerspace (a place for hands-on, inventive, and engaging activities for students), a science room, or large group activity space.

There was a bit of consternation about not having the legacy or old-style cafeteria serving hundreds. The visionary team asked questions like: Where would community groups meet? How would the kitchen work? Where would staff-wide meetings occur? When innovative ideas are presented, it is very common to encounter resistance to change. The district decided to keep the idea on the table and have more conversations with others who would be affected by this monumental change, innovative change. Answers and solutions were contemplated and then implemented.

In the end, the district decided the flex café design idea would be best for the kids, provide the most flexibility of space within a grade wing, and would meet the guiding principles they set out to accomplish. They had a plan, and they stuck to their principles. Each grade wing would be designed with an integrated flex café along with a serving kitchen. The main production kitchen would be located on the first floor and have a servery for each grade level.

The school opened in September 2021. This would be the first time the community, students, and staff would step into the building due to COVID-19; students had been remote learning since the prior school year. Because the school opened while COVID-19 was still flexing its variants, those who visited the building liked the idea of smaller cafés to reduce the number of students in one space. Some even thought the design was conceived due to the pandemic (but all the planning for this project was pre-COVID-19). Construction for this new school started in early spring of 2020, just as the world was shutting down. I have been back to the school several times since its opening, and the principal of the school shared with me that they are using the flex cafés in ways they could never have imagined.

Like the Wright brothers, the Monona Grove School District wanted something innovative, something that they would work to invent and didn't know would work. They were trendsetters; they took a chance and got messy. They asked themselves and their team to think differently about what they knew, and they opened their minds to a different way of thinking, creating something new that others could follow.

Don't be afraid to create something new, something that no one has seen before! This is true innovation. And when the new thingamabob is created, share it! This will spur further innovation. When I started out in the field of architecture as a young twenty-something, I took chances with clients and teams. I was bold and willing to make mistakes; I think it's almost expected that you'll make mistakes. Fresh hires always seem to have more innovative ideas—some great and some not so much. Over time and as I moved up in my profession, I limited if not completely stopped taking chances. I think the further you get into your career the less others are willing to cut you slack for making mistakes or taking chances. It was this lack of getting messy that brought me to the point of thinking I was no longer giving my all. No matter your position, it's ok to make mistakes and get messy. Never stop innovating! It is how we learn and become better at what we do.

CHAPTER 3

PROJECT MANAGEMENT

Be a Management Maverick

Textbooks on project management will explain administrative components, budgets, schedules, contracts, consultants, scope of work or services, resource allocation, and other parts of the process. In its simplest form, there is a project and there are people who must be managed to ensure success, hence the need for a project manager.

Many project management tools are available, such as resource planning and project budgeting software. Understanding and utilizing the tools at hand are vital to being a good project manager, don't get me wrong. Heck, I always looked for ways to improve our project management tools. But I also believe that these tools can be used by anyone, not necessarily just a project manager. What distinguishes a 3PM Leader is the ability to bring a sixth sense to the toolbox: an intuitive knowledge and innate ability to almost predict how to create a successful outcome.

There is a scene in the blockbuster movie, *Top Gun: Maverick*, where Maverick (played by actor Tom Cruise), a decorated naval-aviator-turned-flight-instructor, is standing in front of a dozen or so top gun pilots, presumably the best of the best. He is holding the manual for the F-18 Super Hornet aircraft they fly and presumably know inside and out. Maverick holds up the three-inch-thick manual and asks the pilots if they know everything in the book. The pilots, in typical military response, confidently and boldly reply, "Damn straight! You got it!" Those pilots know the technical capabilities of the aircraft inside and out, its flight characteristics, its weapons systems, and its technical and mechanical systems.

Maverick then takes the large manual and drops it, uncaringly, into the small trash can at his side. There's a breathless pause and confusion ensues. He then says to the pilots, in regard to their limits, "I intend to find them, test them, push beyond. Today we'll start with what you only think you know. You show me what you're made of." And that's what this chapter is about. Discovering who we are and our capabilities as project managers.

3PM Leaders have skills that elevate them to this title. They can see obstacles that are out of sight of others; they have a sense as to what others are feeling without the words being explicitly spoken. They can almost predict the future. These skills aren't learned from a book; they are instilled in us through our life experiences. They are reflections of who we are and the wisdom we have gained. Your values, beliefs and capabilities to navigate tough decisions are what will make you a great 3PM Leader. Are you a 3PM Leader?

- Do you stick with your wingman or leave her to pursue your own glory? Sticking with your wingman means that you are with them to the end, either positive or negative.

You both make a team, and putting the team first could mean the difference between success or failure.

- Do you run out of the burning building or run in to rescue your team? Running to trouble can potentially put you in harm's way, but not rushing in to help your team can spell certain doom for them. Taking on tough issues head-on will instill confidence and trust in your team. They will know you have their backs in times of trouble.

- Do you stick with your team during deadlines? Staying with your team during a deadline, bringing them dinner, for instance, can also build camaraderie and trust. Leaving your team in the throes of a deadline can instill resentment and dissent. It can lead to a lack of respect and trust.

- Do you lighten a teammate's load when the burden is too heavy? Knowing how your teammates are doing physically and emotionally is vital to creating caring connections. A great project manager has an innate sense of these things in themselves and others.

Having these values, beliefs, and capabilities distinguish a great project manager from a good project manager. Understanding your team includes understanding their workload, personal pressures, and skill sets; this enables you to better plan how they will be involved in the project. A health issue, expecting the birth of a child, or being chronically overworked will affect the performance of any person on your project, and it is up to a great project manager to recognize these things and plan accordingly.

Since the project manager is at the forefront of the project process and is the main contact, it is their responsibility to ensure that the project and process go smoothly. When an error occurs on a project, a great project manager will protect the team from the fallout. They will take the heat for the error, apologize for the error, and then get it corrected without throwing the team under the bus.

It's these intangibles, interpersonal skills, or soft skill sets that set great project managers above good project managers. It's not the tool that makes a great project manager or leader, it's who they are as a person.

Set and Meet Expectations

We all have expectations, both of ourselves and of others. Identifying them, writing them down, explaining them, expressing their importance, and then living them helps everyone succeed in meeting expectations. As a leader, you should write a list of each team member and what you expect from them. Not identifying and expressing expectations can lead to unexpected outcomes and disappointment for everyone. I have, at times, not expressed clear expectations for project teams, which led to a kind of wandering by those I was supposed to be leading. Without clear expectations, your people don't really know what you want, when you want it, or even how you want it done. This can lead to disappointment, frustration, anger, and degradation within your team.

While leading one project team, I thought I had clearly communicated the schedule expectation for selecting interior finishes, but as time passed and things were falling behind, I approached my team with the issue. They indicated that I had not clearly communicated the schedule expectation. This lack of communication created frustration and a loss of trust with my team.

When I moved into a studio director position where I would be leading a team of no fewer than twenty-five professionals, I thought it important to outline my team expectations. I also thought it important to express my goals for our studio, as I planned to take our market to new heights and that was going to require everyone to be on board. Change is hard and not everyone is up for it, so I did offer anyone not wanting to join this journey an opportunity to get involved elsewhere in the firm. We all would be the GLUE that binds the team, the client, the project, and the firm together. GLUE: Guide, Listen, and Understand before Engaging (or leading).

My expectations were that we all would be supportive of our teammates and clients by:

Guiding

- We are the experts of what we do
- Guide others/ clients through the process
- Be a mentor to everyone

Listening

- Listen first
- Listen before trying to solve problems
- Recognize unspoken issues

Understanding

- Seek first to understand
- Ask follow-up questions
- Be flexible to different personality types

Engaging

- Lead where appropriate (everyone is a leader regardless of role)

- Maintain a high level of interest in all aspects of the project
- Live the company's mission and value

I also had expectations for each individual team member related to how best to communicate with me, how to evaluate their individual performance, and how we treat our clients. You can think of your staff as the lifeline of your company, and this is CPR to keep things ticking along smoothly.

Communications

- Prefer face-to-face

  Face-to-face communication is better; it adds emotions, body language, and voice inflection to the experience.

- Cell phone call or text (inside and outside of the office)

  Being that I was seldom at my desk, I had my desk phone transfer to my cell phone after a few rings so that I wouldn't miss a call. This also allowed my teammates to reach me wherever I happened to be, either in or out of the office.

- If issues arise (personal, professional, and project/client), address them immediately

  No issue will resolve itself, and seldom does the passing of time make it better. Addressing issues immediately will help improve outcomes.

Performance

- Maintain a good mix of family and work

  Family always comes first. Ensure that there is a good mix of family and work time as an imbalance can be detrimental to both. Understand time will constantly swing in each direction.

- Always plan on projects making a profit

  Have a profitable mindset regardless of the project size, challenges, or fees. Unless you are a non-profit company, you are in the business to make a profit, so ensure it will happen by maintaining mindset.

- Point out and celebrate good performers

  Leaders don't always see what people are doing day in and day out so they may miss an act by someone that needs to be celebrated. It's everyone's job to point out and celebrate good performers.

Respect

- Treat your clients with respect—always

  You may not always get along with the client, but you are representing the firm. Don't allow personal feelings to diminish respect for clients. A change in personnel will be made if an issue can't be overcome.

- Treat your teammates with respect like they are your client

  We are a team, and we work with and for each other.

- Respect the process

  There is a process to be followed on every project, however, understand that not every tool in the process toolchest will be utilized.

These are examples that worked for me; you may need to add or modify. You may have additional expectations for those in leadership roles in your company or on your project team. These should always be written down and expressed, with or without the acronyms, but acronyms do improve the ability to recall expectations and add to clarity when not overused. Your team can't read your mind, and you can't reference or enforce what wasn't emphasized.

Once you've established what you expect from others, make sure the reciprocal happens and there is communication from your team regarding what they expect from you. This was an enlightening concept for me. When I developed my list of expectations of others, I also put myself in their shoes and I expected the same things from me. However, when you ask your team what they expect from you, they may give you points you haven't thought about. For example, I didn't realize how thirsty people would be for real time feedback on their work, either positive or negative. There was an overwhelming need for staff to understand how I and others thought they were doing in the moment.

I can think of times I assumed that my expectations were explicit in the directions I conveyed to a fellow teammate, however, after the task was completed, I was surprised at what was returned. I often thought I had communicated schedule, task-specific details, and outcomes explicitly; however, it was obvious after reviewing the work that I was wrong. Often, we are rushed to move on to the next thing and therefore our instructions are ambiguous. One example of instructions like those we should avoid is when we say we, "Need that as soon as possible." I don't even know what that means! As soon as possible might be someone waiting and standing by your side for you to immediately complete the assigned task, or it can mean in the next day or two. Setting clear expectations on deadlines will help with the success of the task. It is your responsibility as project manager to communicate clear expectations and to be approachable when messages aren't received clearly by your team, your client, or other project leaders.

Use the above examples to create your own list of expectations for your team to be GLUE and to be the lifeline, or use CPR, then ask your team what expectations they have of you. These simple, proactive steps can eliminate ambiguity and create a more trusting environment and, ultimately, a more successful project. Communication truly is key!

Build Relationships

Building strong, long-lasting relationships with your clients and teammates is essential to creating a cohesive team. As a leader, I have had the opportunity to build relationships by bringing people up, not bringing them down, with the words I used, actions I took, or behaviors I showed. Strong relationships require building trust, being dependable, having empathy, being reliable and, for me, must include the ability to have fun. When these actions are ignored or even blatantly opposed, a relationship can become toxic and unsustainable.

It was quite common for my project team members to work well over forty hours in a typical work week for many weeks on end to complete a project and meet a deadline. Unfortunately, this seemed to happen on more and more projects, which I could see was leading to low morale and burnout. I was told to convey to my team that they needed to work more hours to "get over the hump" of present workload needed to complete the project. But how could I tell my already hardworking team that they need to work more hours? How could I absorb the directives and stand down to let them do their work?

I believe that if you hold true to who you are, being aware and not compromising relationships with your team, then you can, as Stephen Covey states in his book *Seven Habits of Highly Effective People*, build trust and loyalty. I chose to let my team work without the pressure or possible negative impact of what upper management wanted me to tell them.

A relationship is a two-way street. It must be amenable for both sides. I have a relationship with my wife, my kids and grandkids, my daughter-in-law, my co-workers, my friends, my pastor, my neighbors, my mom and dad, my sisters, my clients and consultants, and many others. Each one of these relationships is different. Some are intimate, while others are more acquaintance-based. Each relationship requires a certain level of interaction for it to be built or maintained.

Like water, relationships will always drop to the lowest level of force being applied. For instance, if one person in a partnership, be it romantic or business or friendship, isn't applying equal effort, the resulting strength of that relationship is equal to that of the lowest effort given. Sometimes, the *all-in* person may feel slighted or put off by the lack of effort being put in by the other person, while the person who is just so-so may be put off by all the effort the other person is putting in. Each balances the other, and not in a good way if the effort is mismatched. A relationship is like a navigational buoy in the water: The more weight you add to the buoy, the deeper it sits in the water. The more both parties put into a relationship, the deeper and more meaningful it becomes.

While working with one of the largest and oldest national retail clients at the time, I had the opportunity to do projects and travel around the United States. I did projects in: Memphis, Tennessee; Alpharetta, Georgia; Sacramento, California;

Louisville, Kentucky; and remote places like Fort Dodge, Iowa. Most often, my client was traveling with me, which meant that we would spend entire days working closely together and then evenings enjoying a nice dinner and possibly joining one another for a libation or two. I spent years of my life with these people, whom I now call friends. There are other clients, however, who create distance, keep to themselves, and aren't interested in getting to know you on a personal level or being your friend, and that should not offend you. These clients will need a different relationship management style.

My firm had suite tickets at Miller Park (now American Family Field), the Home of the Milwaukee Brewers, which were meant to be used to entertain clients. I had asked my national retail client team and my design team to attend an afternoon game between the Brewers and the Arizona Diamondbacks. This game would go on to be the longest game in Miller Park history at five hours and forty-nine minutes. I don't remember much of the game, although the seventh inning stretch (which is highlighted by the famous sausage race) was performed twice during this seventeen-inning game. After the nearly six-hour-long game, some of us extended the evening by heading out for a night cap. The next day, back in the office, my leader asked how long I was out, being that he had left before the game was over. I told him we went out after the game for a bit. He could not believe that I spent so much time with this client. The difference was that he saw them as our client, and I saw them as my friends. "Are you kidding me?" I thought to myself. A seventeen-inning game won by a walk-off home run and then everyone just goes home? No way—we went out to celebrate and enjoy each other's company as we should have.

You will work with potentially hundreds of people during your career and, while not every client relationship will end up in a lasting friendship, I am certain you will become friends with a few. There will be others you will wish you had never met. The story I share above may be rare, but I hope not uncommon.

It is easy to tell, as a project manager, if someone wants to build a lasting, friendly relationship or if they are just interested in the services you provide. They will reach out to you, spend time with you, enjoy a laugh with you, and really get to know who you are. These relationships are where the joy of your work comes from, where the success and satisfaction of spending your life as a professional comes from, no matter your discipline or field. Look for these relationships, and when you have one, feed it and keep it full! It takes communication and personal interaction. Phone calls, emails, text messages, social get-togethers, lunches, meetings, and a zillion more things.

Even if you detect a particular client doesn't really want a friendship, I still recommend encouraging positive types of interactions because it's always easier working with a friend, or even someone who is a friendly acquaintance, than an adversary.

Communication Is More than the Key

The word communication is defined by Oxford Languages as, "the imparting or exchanging of information or news; a letter or message containing information or news; the successful conveying or sharing of ideas and feelings." Communication happens not just by your words; it also occurs with emotions, body language, and the aura you exude. Personal interaction is the best way to transmit these feelings.

In project management, we often hear people say that for a project to be successful it takes *communication, communication, communication*. I think this is the easy answer, but there are so many other important factors. I agree that communication is the only way to pass on information. However, communication requires an exchange of information. Communication is more than a key; it's a door. This means that both parties have knowledge of the communication, and it is not just through using words. It's the delivery, the tone, and the inflection, whether explicit or implied. Both entities involved must be able to pass through the door of communication freely.

In 1977, NASA launched two space probes into outer space: *Voyager 1* and *Voyager 2*. *Voyagers 1* and *2* were designed to explore our solar system and then go beyond it in search of life. According to NASA's website, each capsule was equipped with a gold-plated copper disc inscribed with a message prepared by Carl Sagan and his team, in case extraterrestrials might discover them, read the instructions on how to use them, and learn of Earth's languages, sounds of life, and music from Mozart to Chuck Berry.

Just because the *Voyagers* have a golden record for other life forms to find and listen to does not mean we have communicated with aliens. It's the same for that important email you sent. Just because you sent it does not mean your message has been received.

Communication is a two-way street, an open or closed door. It requires interaction by both parties. When an email is sent, you have not yet communicated. Once that email is read, that's when communication has occurred. All too often, we send emails, leave voicemails, or mail a letter, and it is assumed that we have informed the recipient. "I have communicated..." is the standard response when asked what level of contact has occurred. We all know what happens when we ass-u-me; the old school explanation is that it makes an ass out of you and me.

A project manager communicates information of all kinds to their teams, including project schedules, client goals, design intent, project fee, and meeting minutes. We also do "soft" communications, like talking to our teams about personal and non-work-related items like family, sports, and the weather. As a project manager, a leader of the team, we are also responsible for communicating difficult conversations. We need to have conversations with those who may be underperforming and help raise them up. We need to have conversations with those who are exceeding expectations and celebrate them! We also need to nudge those out the door who spend too much time at the office.

Even though relationships and communications are two different things, they are related in that each requires effort from both parties. A relationship can't be built without communicating, and communication only occurs when two have knowledge of the same thing. Communicating does not happen without clarity. Improve clarity by expressing clear and concise expectations first.

Plan to Succeed

"If you fail to plan, you plan to fail" – attributed to Benjamin Franklin.

I cannot tell you how many times an impactful mentor of mine, John Miceli, stated this quote. He even had a way of saying it with a nasally, midwestern accent, imitated by everyone who restated the quote. Planning is one of the most important aspects of project management. The plan is the road map everyone will follow to get to the destination—project completion.

Planning in the context of architecture involves project schedules, consideration of construction sequencing and schedule, owner-needed decisions, approvals (owner, local, state, federal), and project budgets. Those not in the architectural field can read this list and see similarities with your field's particulars.

The project plan itself is multi-faceted and can include a project charter outlining the goals of the project, the mission of the project, and any other specific requirements. The plan will have some type of schedule. It will have a budget that has a total fee and how that fee is expected to be utilized throughout the life of the project. A project plan will have a list of resource requirements from people to equipment. All these project plan components should be shared and known by the entire project team so that everyone is pulling in the same direction, towards the same goals.

Project plans could include the following components:

Timeline/Schedule

- A timeline may be created outlining the duration of time the project will take to complete. The timeline may be broken down by phases or milestone events.
- There may be schedules for things like owner decisions, city, state, and federal approvals.
- You may have a schedule outlining monthly billing so a client can better anticipate cash flow for the project.

Resource Management

- Resource management will be utilized to plan and schedule the staff with the skill sets required to complete a project. This portion of a plan will outline the duration of time a person will be involved in a project.

- There may also be physical resources or tools required for a project that will need to be scheduled and budgeted.

Project Requirements

- I refer to this as the project charter. This documents discussions with the owner as to the mission, vision, and goals of a project and may also include specific details like how many students a new school will accommodate.

Scope/Budget

- The scope of work being performed or the product being delivered should be clearly defined to avoid misunderstandings. The scope may also define the quality expectations of the work.

- Every project will have some type of fee that, to some extent, dictates how much time and how many resources can be applied to a project.

Communications

- You may also have a communication plan outlining when meetings will occur, and when and how project information will be made available.

- A feedback loop on satisfaction might be part of your communication plan. The feedback should be obtained from the owner, consultants, and others outside your firm and, when gathered, should be shared with your internal team.

This is the toolbox of the project manager, containing the tools we use to manage a project or process. All the physical tools for the project are in the project manager toolbox. However, like a carpenter or mechanic with a toolbox full of the latest and shiniest tools and gadgets, not understanding how to use them or what they are used for, or when, makes you only a mediocre carpenter or mechanic at best. Having a vision, an understanding, finesse, and Jedi-like knowledge of your field is most important. Then, and only then, will you be able to pick up a tool and use your mastery to create artistry.

Just because I can go into an art store and buy all the materials necessary to paint in no way makes me Rembrandt or even the slightest of artists. I must understand color theory. I must understand composition. I must understand tonality and saturation. I must understand each brush and the strokes they provide. I must understand the mediums that can be added to the paint which can change its viscosity, permanence, and vibrance. Heck, even the canvas needs to be understood (wood, metal, cotton, linen, paper, etc.). Gaining this knowledge takes experience and time which ultimately equates to wisdom.

Project management is the same. There are many tools you can use; however, the real secret is understanding who you are, who your team is, and all aspects of the field you are in. This is where the magic, the artistry of project management comes in. This is where having gained wisdom elevates you to greatness. These skills and knowledge can be learned, but it really comes down to who you are and your willingness to adjust who you are to be the best 3PM Leader possible. Adjust to the canvas, the brushes, and the paint that you are provided.

For proper planning, each project should start with a project charter. The project charter documents the vision, goals, and requirements for a project. This is the road map that, if followed, will provide for a successful project and will help inform a project plan. This information is best gathered at the project kick-off meeting in some type of word processing software such as Microsoft Word. This should be a living document and be reviewed at important milestones to confirm the vision, goals and requirements are being adhered to. As the client makes categorical changes, the project charter should be updated and reshared with the entire project team.

A project should also have a project plan with the schedule and a list of resources (including personnel) needed for the duration of the project, from start to completion. When I say completion, that includes the turning over of the keys to the owner. Other things that make up a project plan include a fee that is based on the schedule, the work effort required to complete the project, and resources needed.

Once the plan is established, it should be shared with your team. Having a road map of where one is going is vital to ensure that everyone is moving in the same direction and for the same purpose. When I talk about sharing the plan, I mean the *entire* plan. Financial aspects of the plan must be communicated to the team so they have a clear understanding of budgets and profit expectations, otherwise there is a less likely chance these will be met. Project schedules, including a resource schedule, should be shared so the team has a clear understanding of their expected time commitment.

Even with a plan, things don't always go accordingly, and this is where project managers must model flexibility. Just like your typical day, there are always unexpected things that come up, needing to be addressed, that deviate from your project plan. The most well thought out calendar still accommodates the unexpected, and a project plan is just like that. It must have contingencies built in for the unexpected. Remember, it's a plan, and plans often change, however there must be one in place.

I was in the throes of construction administration of a new school in a public school district. The current school district superintendent was heavily involved in the project process and set the direction for almost everything. They determined the level of innovation that would be incorporated into the building down to the finishes in the restrooms. There was also the buildings and grounds director who made decisions based on their own individual experiences with building systems and a business manager who made sure we were on budget.

During the construction process, it was announced that the superintendent would be retiring. Shortly thereafter, the business manager and the buildings and grounds director would also announce that they were leaving the school district! Everyone involved in the decision-making process for this project from the owner's side were leaving and would be replaced by new teammates. This meant that the entire owner leadership team was changing. These new teammates would have no history with the project and no input on decisions that had already been made.

The first thing I did was not panic. I considered what information the new team would need, what owner decisions had been made, and which ones were still needed. I coordinated a meeting with the new leadership team, and we met to review and relaunch everything. Items like project mission, owner requirements, the project team and their roles, key issues still outstanding, project schedule (from start to completion), and project budget were re-introduced. Then it was time to take questions from the new owner team. I also had to adjust my time on the project so I could spend more time with the new team members to bring them up to speed.

Nothing ever goes exactly as planned and, because of this, contingencies need to be built into the project plan. This may mean more time for the project, a bit more budget to get the work done, or lightening the workload of staff to allow for time on these contingencies. If your calendar is full and inflexible, you will not be able to pivot when, and I say *when*, change happens.

When planning a project, you can take some steps to anticipate key issues that may affect your project plan with thorough knowledge of…

- Your client and their knowledge of the process. If this is the first time your client has designed and built a new building, for instance, you should anticipate that more guidance will be required.

- Your team's experience. Having a veteran team might mean a project gets done more efficiently, while a new or rookie team might need more guidance.

- Project waypoints. These are things like approvals, decision making processes and project requirements. Each of these may have steps that take more time than anticipated.

Abraham Lincoln once said, "Give me six hours to chop down a tree and I will spend the first four hours sharpening the axe." This is basically saying: invest time in preparation and it will pay off in the end. There are studies out there that say an hour of planning can save 20 - 200 hours of corrective rework.

Success comes when a project is well thought-out, has the right amount and type of resources, and the scope is well defined. Projects succeed and fail for a multitude of reasons; at any point along the journey there is an assessment of current conditions and a stopping point, or a point where a change of course can take place that will affect the outcome. It takes a good project manager to recognize that something is awry, but it takes a great 3PM Leader to recognize it and do something about it.

Stay Fearless

Fear can prevent us from experiencing new things, finding new opportunities, and being innovative. As I became more entrenched in my career and organization, I felt like it could all go away with one wrong move, and I became more cautious. It's the Ivory Tower effect—you stop to look down from what you've built yourself up to and become overprotective and less risky, so nothing comes crashing down. I was fearful of crossing thresholds.

I was playing building blocks with my granddaughter the other day—you know, the red, blue, yellow, orange, square, rectangular, round-shaped ones. We were going to build towers to see how high we could build them. Of course, she wanted hers to reach to the clouds! We started out building our own towers in our own world. I had gotten to a third level of blocks when I looked at hers; she had lain a bunch of red, flat blocks on the carpet which would give hers a solid foundation. I started mine with thin, square blocks laid flat with longer red blocks set on top—these would be the columns. I took the column and beam approach (after all, I am an architect). At first, we added blocks with little thought of collapse, but as we got taller and taller we were more cautious of the steps we took with the pieces we added and where we added them. We would study the lean of the structure and decide to place the next block slightly off-center to help counter the lean. Always looking to go higher with the next block, we cautiously added to our leaning tower until, yes, as always happens, it came crashing down.

Building the block tower reminded me of my career and how I seemed to get more cautious as I moved through and up. It's often said the higher you are, the longer the fall. I did not want to fall, and therefore I became more cautious. I wonder now if this held me back from doing my best.

As a GenX-er, the early days of simpler living when I grew up allowed kids to be more independent and riskier than today's generation. I'm not saying our generation was better, just that, because of social and societal change (and even parenting dynamics), today's generations seem less comfortable with managing reasonable risk. We didn't have helicopter parents that watched over everything we did; they didn't come to every school event, and they didn't know where we were every hour of every day, which meant, to a degree or until we lost it, they invested trust in us. When my son and daughter were in school and had parts in their high school musical, we went to every, and I mean *every* performance. I know other parents who will stress themselves out to be present at every single event, even to the detriment of their own health; if they don't, they would consider themselves bad parents. To some extent, helicopter parenting has prevented kids from taking risks, learning risk-tolerance, and respecting boundaries.

My generation was allowed, to some extent, to manage our own risk. We could ride our bikes to the edge of the city if we were comfortable. We could walk to the grocery store, a local ball diamond, and stay out past dark all with our parents trust- ing we would manage our own risk. We were still on a leash, but our parents extended it beyond where they could see. If we failed at managing ourselves, our parents would pull us back and, in some cases, ground us.

These experiences of supported independence helped mold my self-esteem and confidence. I believed that I could do anything if I set my mind to it. I could ride my bike miles to downtown, I could be gone from home all day with my friends, I could handle a paper route on my own in the dark. The people in my life—family, friends, and co-workers—all added something to making me, me. Project management is managing risk. We risk not meeting a schedule, not meeting a budget, not meeting client expectations. Risk is inherent in every aspect of what we do. These early experiences, like those you may have benefited from, were preparing us.

A 3PM Leader must be fearless for ultimate success and longevity. This fearlessness must be there when evaluating risk, picking a direction, and making decisions. Leaders can't be afraid to make mistakes; we must be fearless in confronting dif- ficult conversations since some of the best, leading to the most successful outcomes, started out being the ones we wished to avoid. Leaders must have a get-it-done attitude, always push- ing forward for what is right to elevate all involved. The best project managers have a fearless attitude and are always ready to jump into the lion's den.

If you are feeling that you have become complacent or more fearful of taking chances or innovating, think back to the concept of getting messy. It's ok to get messy, come up with new ideas, and experiment with a new process or tool. Without taking a chance and crossing a threshold into the unknown, we may not find out what is truly possible and what we are capable of. Stay fearless!

Lessons Learned

We don't fail, we learn to do something different the next time. The quote, "Success is not final, failure is not fatal: it is the courage to continue that counts", (attributed first to Winston Churchill), epitomizes this concept. There is typically not one thing leading to a project's failure or success. Most of the time there is a series of events strung together that, if left to keep going in a negative direction, often leads to failure or disappointment. Break this chain of events as soon as you can to maximize project success.

Consider if an owner asks for a small change to a project, and you decide not to charge for the additional service, for instance. An additional service is anything outside the agreed upon, contracted scope of work. You also didn't tell the client this was an additional service, and you weren't going to charge them for it. This would be a freebie. Maybe this happens a few more times, and you continue ignoring the "freebie" to the point that you realize your fee, or your profit, is at risk. You go back to the owner asking for additional services for changes that were asked for months ago, and the client starts to feel that you are "nickel-and-diming" them. This reminds me of the adage, "No good deed goes unpunished." This outcome could have been avoided by notifying the owner of the additional services you were not charging for but that, at some point, they may have to pay in terms of future changes. Eliminating the small surprises will eliminate the progression of a bad situation.

I am a pilot, and I fly for fun. Just like anything, being a pilot and flying requires work to keep the saw sharp. When aviation accidents occur, it usually is not related to one thing, but rather a chain of events. If the chain is broken and action is taken to adjust a mindset, an action, or an attitude, there will most likely be a better outcome. Some accidents happen when pilots fly into conditions requiring them to rely upon instruments and the pilot is not certified or capable of doing so. The simple act of turning the plane 180 degrees out of the instrument conditions can save lives. There are attitudes that get pilots in trouble, and I think they are applicable to our discussion here as well. The Federal Aviation Administration (FAA) lists five hazardous attitudes that can undermine a pilot's aeronautical decision-making. They are: antiauthority, impulsivity, invulnerability, macho, and resignation. The FAA defines these as:

Antiauthority

This attitude is found in people who do not like anyone telling them what to do. In a sense, they are saying no one can tell them what to do. They may be resentful of having someone tell them what to do or may regard rules, regulations, and procedures as silly or unnecessary. However, it is always your prerogative to question authority if you feel it is in error.

Strategy to overcome: Follow the rules—they are usually right!

Impulsivity

The attitude of people who frequently feel the need to do something—anything—immediately. They do not stop to think about what they are about to do, they do not select the best alternative, and they do the first thing that comes to mind.

Strategy to overcome: Stop, think, consider—then act.

Invulnerability

Many people feel that accidents happen to others, but never to them. They know accidents can happen, and they know that anyone can be affected. They never really feel or believe that they will be personally involved. Pilots who think this way are more likely to take chances and increase risk.

Strategy to overcome: Have an attitude that it *can* happen to me.

Macho

Pilots who are always trying to prove that they are better than anyone else are thinking, "I can do it—I'll show them!" Pilots with this type of attitude will try to prove themselves by taking risks to impress others. While this pattern is thought to be a male characteristic, women are equally susceptible.

Strategy to overcome: Taking chances is foolish.

Resignation

Pilots who think, "What's the use?" do not see themselves as being able to make a great deal of difference in what happens to them. When things go well, the pilot is apt to think that's good luck. When things go badly, the pilot may feel that someone is out to get them or attribute it to bad luck. The pilot will leave the action to others, for better or worse. Sometimes, such pilots will even go along with unreasonable requests just to be a "nice guy."

Strategy to overcome: I'm not helpless, I can and need to act and make a difference.

These attitudes outlined by the FAA can also be seen every day in the workplace and in project managers and leaders. As you were reading them, were you applying names and faces to them, possibly even your own? Understanding and identifying issues that might get you in trouble and having strategies on how to get out of them by breaking the chain of events can lead to better outcomes.

Tap Into Your Well-Rounded Knowledge

Being well-rounded means you have filled in the voids in a wide-angle view. The voids are those gaps in between and around the edges of what we know. Filling in the voids means that you have a comprehensive understanding of your profession or process. Everything, regardless of what it is, has a process and that process has steps or components. When we only have knowledge of a few of these steps and we don't have knowledge of the step in between the ones we know, we don't have a complete understanding. Having knowledge of all the steps, having filled the voids of what we didn't know, gives us well-rounded knowledge. Having well-rounded knowledge of everything that goes into your profession gives you a better understanding of the entire process of what you do and adds to your armamentarium of skills to deal with any situation that may arise on your projects.

The process of architecture has phases or steps that include pre-design, schematic design, design development, construction documentation, and construction administration. Prior to a building being constructed, there are many approvals that need to be obtained, and each has its own specific processes. A well-rounded knowledge will help you understand when these approvals are needed and how best to obtain them.

During the planning process for a new building, architects often must obtain building and site design approvals from the local planning commission. This approval process can be daunting with all the information required and the deadlines for submittal of information. I have found that having pro-active meetings with the local official to review the planning commission approval process, required submittal information, and timing of the submittal ensures clear understanding and smooth process. Being mentored by others taught me how to intentionally make this process go smoothly with pre-submittal meetings.

My son was a Boy Scout and, I am proud to say, he made it to Eagle Scout! I participated in many Scout outings, including one that took place every year during the cold, dark Wisconsin winter months—the Winter Jamboree. Winter days in Wisconsin have limited daylight, which meant that the Boy Scout events finished about 4 p.m., leaving a lot of time for us to spend in our cabins preparing meals and playing games. This outing typically had over twenty boys and at least six adult leaders.

One evening after dinner, one of the leaders, Mr. K, was playing a game not on his phone but from one of those paperback game books. I asked what the game was, and he said it was sudoku. Sudoku is a nine-by-nine grid puzzle divided into three-by-three boxes. Every row, column, and box must contain the numbers one through nine, with no repeats. It looked simple enough, so I gave it a try. I understood the game concept, but there was a void in my understanding of how to play the game. I struggled for a bit with really no understanding of what I was doing, even though I knew the concept of completing the puzzle.

Mr. K saw me struggling and filled my knowledge gap. He shared a strategy on how to figure out what number went where. Once he showed me his technique, I could almost see the puzzle solved in my head. I won't be entering the World Sudoku Championship, but the newfound knowledge did fill a gap and made me a well-rounded sudoku player.

To be able to piece together, to be able to better answer and provide leadership to a team, one must have knowledge and understand all steps or components and their intricacies. It's like the old phrase, "Jack of all trades, but a master of none,"—only you are a master of your professional process. This doesn't mean that you are a "know it all," it does mean, however, that you have an understanding, you know all the important steps, and you know where to go for information and answers requiring expertise that you don't have.

By having a well-rounded knowledge of your profession and everything that accompanies it, you can see the big picture, see how things are connected, why they are connected, and plan so as not to break a link or misstep. When you can see the big picture of all the components, you can see oncoming issues and problem solve much easier.

Be Humble

Having humility is freedom from pride or arrogance and knowing your skills and flaws. Having humility allows you to share freely and put others ahead of yourself. It allows you to give authentic praise and gratitude where deserved and, I would also say, required. Being humble also shows others that you can be forgiving and can be open to ideas other than your own. Humility comes with wisdom, which takes time and life experience. Having humility is critical when dealing with your team and your clients, as they run the spectrum from dominating and demeaning to supportive and collaborative.

Humility is important when leading teams. As the leader or project manager, you may not know everything, you may not have all the answers. This is why you have a team. Having humility to understand this and allowing others to rise above you can be difficult but is required to build new leaders. Allow yourself humility to authentically pass on praise, responsibility, and the spotlight. You will be surprised how this will make a difference in someone's life.

I'm a Star Wars fan, not one of those fanatics who easily recite every stormtrooper's number or other minute obscure detail, but a basic fan. Luke Skywalker, the young man in Episode IV (let's not start a debate on episode numbering) is someone with dreams and a drive to do what he wants to do regardless of what others who have more knowledge and wisdom are advising him. Luke is arrogant and overconfident. He meets Obi-Wan Kenobi who, unbeknownst to Luke, is a real-life Jedi master. As we watch Episodes V and VI, we see Luke go from a wild, unpredictable young man to a mature, confident Jedi. He has gained wisdom through the experiences with his Jedi master, Obi-Wan. Luke has found humility through wisdom. Eventually Luke, who honed his skills while being mentored by a Jedi master, becomes a Jedi master and, in turn, shows others the Jedi way. It was Obi-Wan's humility, his openness to share his knowledge, that allowed Luke to gain the wisdom to become a Jedi Master. Are you a Jedi Master waiting to share your superpowers or are you on the path to the dark side wanting to tightly grasp control and power like Anakin Skywalker?

I had my own Obi-wan mentor, John Miceli. John was a mild-mannered, soft spoken, gentle leader who gave freely of his time, knowledge, and wisdom. When I first started working with John, I thought I had a good grasp of the architectural process and working with clients, but I wanted more! I wanted to take the next step in leading clients and becoming their trusted advisor. John and I ended up on many projects together, and I benefitted and learned from the great relationships he had built. John took time to introduce me to those clients and eventually gave me tasks to do that would start to instill trust between the client and me. I was allowed to create agendas for meetings and then lead the meetings. I created presentation content for board meetings and presented the information.

John openly and graciously shared his knowledge and was not threatened by others. Prior to school board presentations, John would ask me if I wanted to present, and I immediately jumped at the chance. Then, as I gained more experience and confidence, he would ask if he needed to be at a meeting or if I could handle it on my own. Again, I took that opportunity to go alone. John always followed up with me to see how things went, but he had put his trust in me to do the right thing. I was not the only person who John allowed these career advancement opportunities; he did this with most everyone. John saw the bigger picture. He knew that his knowledge and wisdom needed to be passed on to others so they could fill his shoes someday. I am forever thankful for the trust John gave me and the attitude to share it forward.

An architect designs a custom, one-of-a-kind building that most likely will only be built once. Think of it as a one-of-a-kind prototype. Typically, prototypes are not perfect, and adjustments will need to be made during the building of it. While working with John, I saw him approach these issues with humility. He told clients at the onset that this was a one-of-a-kind building, it had never been designed or built before, and that he had never produced a perfect set of drawings and most likely never would. He humbly set the expectation that he was not perfect, and perfection should not be the expectation.

What I learned from John was that it's not bad to respectfully challenge a client. It's good to be up front with a client in setting realistic expectations. It's not bragging to share your experience and expertise. It's your responsibility to admit when a mistake is made and to make it right. John was a master at emotional intelligence, and I was able to absorb that and internalize it to a point that I could also use it to my advantage. If you don't have a mentor with superpowers that you also want to have, then seek that person or persons out.

Early in my career, I was ambitious for knowledge and experiences. I wanted to understand everything about what I was doing and the process which it followed and needed. Once I got my professional license and had worked in the profession for three years, I thought I had a pretty good understanding of the process of architecture. I felt I knew it all.

I started to explore other certifications that would build on my knowledge base. One of those certifications was available through the Construction Specifications Institute (CSI); they have three levels of certification, and the first one is the Construction Document Technologist (CDT). This seemed like a simple certification to get since I had a "great" understanding of construction documents and the architectural process.

I signed up to attend study sessions that would occur on Saturday mornings for several weeks. The study sessions would prepare us to take the certification exam. The classes were hosted at a local company. Walking into what looked like a training room, I was greeted by a room full of others who had signed up for these classes. My fellow classmates appeared to be about my age, which I equated to the same experience level. The class syllabus would follow the table of contents of the Manual of Practice or, as one of our instructors called it, the MOP. This was the CSI Bible of the architectural process— the clear, correct and concise process. Reading the table of contents, my confidence started building. The topics covered included construction documents (I had been doing these for years) and specifications (I had written tons of these). I knew that I knew this stuff; after all, I had been doing it for years—I had experience!

Our instructor was well known and well respected in the local architecture community. He had a big personality and thick German accent. He started talking about project phases and I was like, blah blah blah, I know this stuff. He then showed us an image of the actual items that we produce, the drawings, the specifications, the contracts, the bidding information, addenda, etc. and he told us that not all of these were part of contract documents. Wait, what did he say? Contract documents? I had not heard that term before… did he mean construction documents? As he proceeded showing us a graphic representation of the process of what we did and how the pieces fit together, I suddenly felt like I had walked into the wrong room. He was talking about things that I hadn't heard before and didn't understand. This reminded me of my college days when you walked into a lecture hall on the first day of class and the professor pointed to the class title she had written on the board, saying, "If this is not the class you signed up for, you are in the wrong room," and suddenly a handful of people walk out. I felt like I was in the wrong room and should walk out. What our German accented instructor was saying was completely foreign to me and it wasn't because of his accent. It was mind-blowing; I suddenly realized I did not know everything, even though I had been practicing architecture for years! I was a licensed architect; I passed a weeks' worth of tests telling me so, yet I didn't really know or understand the process of architecture. At this point my confidence in my knowledge and understanding was shaken and I hoped it was not recognizable by the others in the class.

I had been doing the things needed to complete the process of architecture for years, but I wasn't necessarily doing them in the correct order, nor understanding the importance or nonimportance of a particular part of the documentation or process. When I got home, I told my wife of this humbling experience. Even though I was humbled, I was even more hungry and excited for the next class. I wanted to learn more. I wanted to understand better the process of what I was doing on a day-to-day basis. I wanted a thorough and complete understanding of the profession I was in.

Monday morning came and I headed to work excited to share the information and knowledge I had gained. Could I be the only one who didn't know this stuff? I soon realized that several of my teammates didn't know this stuff either, some who had been in architecture longer than me. After the study sessions were complete, I took the test for Construction Document Technologist certification and passed. I felt I had a thorough understanding of the process of architecture and was ready to share this knowledge with others. And share I did—and still do today.

Going through this process of certification gave me an understanding of where liabilities lay and gave me the tools to help position my projects and teams for success. Throughout my career I would share information from the MOP to aspiring architects and some seasoned architects. I would share best practices and help others with their understanding of the process of architecture. It's been almost thirty years since getting the CDT certification and I often refer others to the MOP and share sections of the book.

I think most professionals can identify with the idea that there is a correct way, a correct order for the process of what they do. I also believe that those same professionals, if they have a thorough understanding of their professions process, see disorder in it by others. It's the responsibility of those who have a thorough understanding of the process to share the correct process and redirect others who misstep. We, as 3PM leaders and project managers, must adopt a lifestyle of showing humility and learning from others, then informing and leading when appropriate.

CHAPTER 4

PROCESS MANAGEMENT

Understand the Process—Thoroughly!

Tap...Tap...Tap! The maestro's baton quickly taps the top of their music stand readying the orchestra. Project management, what project managers do, can be compared to being a maestro. The maestro of an orchestra is highly knowledgeable in the art of music. They are masters at reading complex musical scores. The maestro choreographs a musical score to ensure melodic harmonies. They help bring in instrumentalists when the piece of music calls for them and sometimes ask more or less from them— crescendo and decrescendo. The maestro shows emotion they want the music to emulate. They are responsible for timing, bringing in instrumentalists when needed, and letting them go when not. They help maintain the feeling and the emotion required for the piece of music that will leave a lasting emotional impression on the audience.

A maestro may have the ability to play an instrument or two but almost certainly doesn't have the knowledge or ability to play all instruments. However, they do have a complete and thorough understanding of the sounds, qualities, and timbre instruments produce. With a thorough understanding of the art of music, the sounds instruments emanate, the maestro guides musicians through a process of creating a beautifully interlaced musical score into a wide-ranging sound, forever intertwined, that hangs in the symphony hall.

Project managers are maestros of the process of our profession. We have a thorough understanding of the process of what we do, however we are not masters of every component. We are responsible for project timing, establishing a project team, and setting the tone, mood, and rhythm to the process, as well as the goals of the project. We know when to bring in new team members and when to let them go. With this wide-ranging and thorough knowledge of our profession, we can guide our teams through the process of creating something beautiful.

For project managers to gain experience and have a thorough understanding, they need to be involved in every aspect of the project. Project managers should be involved in the pre-proposal walkthroughs, RFP strategies, project interviews, establishing teams, performing the work, and the post-project review. They must understand the intricacies laced between the big chunks of what we do.

Typically on architectural projects, there is a team of members doing most of the work of architecture, which includes: creating the design; turning that design into construction documents that will be utilized by a construction company to build the building; construction administration during construction and shop drawing review; reviewing requests for interpretation; issuing construction bulletins, along with many other duties. The project manager must have a thorough understanding of this entire process, or things can go astray. Team members are experts in their role, but they may lack a complete and thorough understanding of the process. The project manager, with their complete understanding, must guide, monitor, and redirect when necessary to maintain the proper direction of the entire process.

When a Request for Proposal comes in the door, a PM should be assigned so the administrative aspect of a project can begin. Project numbers must be created, review of RFP for scope and services need to be identified, skill sets needed for the project must be identified, cost-benefit analysis determined, and ability to complete the project evaluated as defined by the RFP and many other tasks.

Understanding the process of what you are doing will allow you to put the pieces together in the right order, at the right time, and with the right people in the right role. This is true in whatever you are managing. Understanding (not necessarily being an expert at each component but *understanding*) each step is vital to managing and leading a process.

Throughout my career, I have managed the architectural process. The process has specific steps that must happen before the next step can be taken. This is typical on every project. Project teams can be made up of people who are new to a profession or who have decades of experience. In both cases, the amount of experience is not necessarily an indicator of understanding of the process.

Securing the Perfect Pizza

How do you like your pizza? Which toppings are your favorites, and which ones make you say "eww"? Think of all the options available—the types of pizza (Margherita, Neapolitan,

Marinara, Hawaiian, etc.), all the toppings (pineapples, anchovies, olives, and on and on) and crust options (stuffed, thin, hand tossed). It's mouthwatering to think about all the tasty options.

In your mind, when you place your pizza order, you have designed the perfect pizza, exactly the way you like it. It has everything you want on it—nothing more, nothing less. Once you've ordered the perfect pizza, that is what you are expecting. Have you ever opened the pizza box, and, to your chagrin, it wasn't what you ordered? I have.

Now imagine, rather than a pizza, you're ordering a new building or a new product. Think of all the options available to you: shape, size, exterior finishes, interior finishes, furniture, and on and on. There are literally thousands of options and choices when it comes to design.

When participating in a building project, the owner will be responsible for selecting the toppings they want on the pizza or building. What is the purpose, mission, vision for the building? The answers to these questions provide the ingredients for the building that fits the owner's needs specifically and that the project manager needs to convey to their project team.

Designing a building is like ordering a pizza. Architects take your order and make the pizza to your specifications. Moving through a building project, if you are involved from the inception of the project, you will understand most, if not all, the selections and decisions that are made.

To avoid pizza disappointment by both you and your client, I recommend these steps:

1. Understand what is being ordered. Have you gone to a restaurant and not understood a menu item? I can tell

you when I first saw the word "anchovies" on a pizza menu, I was clueless. If I had not sought understanding, I may have had a very strong and unexpected fishy and salty result.

Asking questions to better understand what is being asked for is vital to meeting expectations. The project manager needs to ask questions to help clarify and better understand any ambiguities presented by the client to ensure proper direction is being taken.

2. Understand who is ultimately ordering and paying for the pizza. It is common for a client to be comprised of a team of individuals who will provide input, but don't necessarily have the authority to provide direction or make decisions.

   Identify decision-makers at the kickoff meeting—identify who will make decisions and about which items. The foundation of any pizza—the crust—is like building systems that support everything else. The toppings are the finishes of a building. Determine who will be responsible for making each of these decisions. It is important to have answers to these questions before starting a project.

3. Don't make assumptions on toppings. Just because you like onion on your pizza, doesn't mean the owner does, so don't put it on the pizza. It is the project manager's role to ascertain what the owner wants on their pizza—nothing more, nothing less.

   However, we do have the responsibility to guide and inspire the owner. Think of this as upselling. If we think the pizza could be better by adding or changing something, we should let the owner know. The owner has hired us for our expertise, and they are relying on us to provide it, so offer up your opinions, but don't add anything without getting the owner's approval first.

4. Verify the order. Okay, you just successfully took the order. At this point, the pizzaiolo repeats back your order, the project requirements, to assure expectations are met. The review of a building project order comes in the form of drawings and specifications that capture the owner's order.

    Now is the time to review the order. You should take time to review the project with the owner. This review should include the project charter and other documents that have outlined previous decisions.

5. Keep an itemized receipt. There are thousands of decisions made over potentially years during the design process—dozens of meetings to discuss choices, choices tracked with meeting minutes. Keep those meeting minutes in order and handy to monitor decisions that have been made.

    It is possible that during the project a client may think they ordered one thing and are getting something else. By having your documentation in order and available, you will be able to address any concerns of the owner.

As an architectural project manager, or any other type of project manager, we help owners work through their ideas to develop a building or reach a goal. The architect interprets what the owner wants through their extensive conversations and provides guidance. The architect works to provide a project that fits best with what the owner has ordered—nothing more and nothing less—but offering up ideas such as these can help guide the owner and ensure they are getting what they ordered.

It's the project manager's role to ensure that the team is always providing what the owner wants. If the project manager is not involved in the entire process, others not as familiar with the order will make decisions leading to unpleasant surprises for everyone when the pizza box is opened.

Things Take Time

Remember the "three Ts"—Things Take Time. Doing work takes time. Planning a project takes time. Thinking takes time! Often, it seems that people forget that things take time, especially today, when people want what they want, when they want it. Who likes waiting more than a minute in a drive through line? A minute is a long time. As the project manager, however, it's your job to manage the expectation of time.

Working with the public in general (public-school projects, specifically) required me to manage expectations of timing. Most often, to pay for a capital improvement project like building a new school, a referendum for funding by voters is needed. Inevitably, once a referendum passed, people both within and outside an organization would ask when construction was to start. The process of creating documents to build a new school or renovate an existing school can take a team a year or more to create once the referendum is approved. Generally, school districts don't have the money to pay for complete sets of documentation prior to the approval of a referendum, so the process of design and documentation occurs secondary to a referendum being approved. However, most people want to smell the flowers right away.

One of my hobbies is photography, and I am always mesmerized by timelapse photography. What I find fascinating is watching the development of a seed into a flower. Entire weeks, if not months, of development are condensed into a few seconds. This technology allows us to see things develop before our eyes. We see progress from seed to complete blooming flower in seconds; we don't have to wait weeks for the fruit of our labors.

One must plant the seed before one can smell the flower. To smell the flower, time must pass, and work must be done. The growth of a flower can take weeks, if not months. There are five stages of development for most flowers; the very first step is to place the seed in fertile soil. Once planted, the seed begins to germinate by taking nutrients from the soil to initiate its start. After four or five days, the germinated seed sends out roots to better gather nutrients and to provide a firm foundation to support the stem and flower. Next, the stem emerges from the seed and starts to burrow through the soil to reach daylight; eventually, leaves develop and use photosynthesis to provide nutrients to the plant. Stage four sees the development of buds on the stem structure. Then finally, after an entire month, a flower opens with the progression of other buds opening over several days.

A project is very similar to the development of a flower in that it takes time to get things done, and these things can't be rushed. Even with plants, compromising what is needed to develop a "standard" plant will have an effect. During the development of the seed into a flower, the plant absorbs water through its roots and leaves over the duration of its life.

Imagine if all the needed water, all the water a plant absorbs during development over several months, was added on day one, when the seed is planted, and no other water was provided for the duration of the growth process. The seed might be washed away in the flood, or it might start to develop roots and a stem structure but will die because the flood of water evaporates and no water is available for further development.

What if we were truly able to reduce the amount of time it took for the plant to bring us a beautiful flower? If we reduced the plant's growth process, it would be detrimental to the plant itself. Rapid growth of plants reduces the overall life expectancy of the plant because carbon cannot be stored in sufficient amounts. Our impatience would kill the plant, and it would be impossible to detail all the times throughout history when impatience killed other things—plans, hopes, dreams.

Ultimately, things take time, and if you rush something, a compromise will happen. Reducing time means something will get less attention and possibly not turn out the way it's expected. In terms of promised quality, you will put the time in one way or another. It is always better if the time is spent intentionally on successfully completing each phase of a process versus rushing, then having to put the time into redesigning, rebuilding, or repairing a damaged client relationship.

I worked with a fantastic project architect, Mark Haberman. Mark understood that things take time and would often compare the process of a project to the development of an embryo into a baby. He used the example well. If time is reduced in the development of an embryo, there might be deficiencies that will have a long-term effect. When a baby is born prematurely, not given the benefit of a full-term pregnancy, there can be complications, some of which last a lifetime.

He also used the example of baking a cake. If you want to get the cake done in half the time and you cook it at double the recommended baking temperature, you will end up with a baked cake, however there will be compromises. The very center might be perfectly done, however the edges and area surrounding the center might be charred to a crisp.

Often, our construction partners condescendingly questioned why we couldn't get our drawings done faster. My typical response was, "Why can't you get the building done faster? Just double the construction crew to get it done in half the time." Their unspoken response was just like mine—things take time. It takes time for concrete to cure. It takes time for creative thinking. Heck, it takes time just for an owner to make decisions.

Allow the process the time it needs and calm down when you get anxious for completion. Ask yourself why, where the need to rush is coming from? Are you being pressured internally or externally? Then always do what is right, which generally is whatever it takes to get a job done correctly. What are you rushing toward? It will not be as satisfying as the completion of a project done according to schedule and plan. We all have rushed something and have regretted it. Measure twice and cut once. There are a lot of examples of why taking the right amount of time is the right thing to do.

All Aboard!

Ah, the quintessential family road trip. My family's road trips consisted of my wife and I and our two kids piled into the minivan. The family road trip always included a starting point, an end point, and plenty of stops in between. Months of careful planning occurred prior to departure: each traveler knew where we were going, what their specific role was, and what was expected of them. Some of the expectations were discussed while others were implied and unspoken. Some of the responsibilities were also discussed, and again, others were unspoken. We just knew that dad filled the gas tank while mom washed the windshield, and the kids collected the accumulated trash. I was also responsible for bringing the pretzel sticks.

Now imagine being in the middle of your road trip, the journey you are on, trading one of your road trippers with someone completely new to the journey. Imagine their potential confusion and bewilderment trying to comprehend how you reached this specific point. Imagine the questions they might ask. Among the first might be, *Where are we? What is the destination? What is my role on this journey? Who are these people with me and what are they doing? Are there roadblocks ahead? Did someone bring pretzels?!*

During several projects, I have experienced personnel change. Client decision-makers have changed. Superintendents, business managers, and buildings and grounds directors all have either retired or left for another district. I have had internal team members change due to project workload or expertise that was needed elsewhere. These personnel changes can result in confusion, surprise and bewilderment. When new team members are added to a project in progress, there is a gap in knowledge, and they may question decisions that have already been made. They don't understand how we got to this point.

The confusion occurs due to a gap in understanding of project decisions and information. The questions asked by our newly added road-trippers are the same types of questions that arise throughout the entire process. However, most of the questions being asked were answered months if not years earlier prior to the new team member joining the journey. A new team member may want to change direction slightly or completely. A new team member may not agree with previous decisions, and they strongly believe a change to the plan is warranted.

A 3PM Leader will onboard new project team members as they are added along the journey. There are four critical steps that need to occur during team member transitions to fill their information gap, avoid confusion, misunderstandings, and consider possible changes.

1. Share the big picture. Ensure that the new team member understands the project plan, including project vision, requirements, schedules and goals. Now is a good time to review the project charter with them.

   Sharing and reviewing the entire project plan will give the newly added team member a wide view of the project's overall roadmap. Having a clear view of where the journey started and where it is going is vital for new team members.

2. Help them find their seat. Before a team member can be effective in their new role, they need to understand how they fit into the project team and what is expected of them. It might also be necessary to adjust the seating chart to better align with what the new team member brings to the team.

   Often, the shoes that have been vacated will not perfectly fit the new member and there will need to be some adjustments made. A new team member's skill set, expectations and vision may be different from what was discussed when the project first kicked off, so be sure to modify the journey if possible and necessary.

3. Inform them how we got to this point. Anyone joining a project midstream has missed many waypoints. The turns your team has taken at various forks in the journey may not make sense until they understand all the variables that led to those decisions. It is essential to share the journey's waypoints—the milestones, decisions, achievements, roadblocks, and potential challenges ahead.

   Having knowledge of why something is the way it is will help move past possible consternation. A slowdown in the supply chain of materials may have caused a substitution that normally would not have been made. This will be questioned by the new team member. Having the knowledge of why that change was made will help them move past this point.

4. Be open to modifying the plan. Sometimes when a new team member is added, there may be reason to alter the plan slightly or even change the destination completely. Think about this as exiting the freeway to jump on the parallel frontage road or set out on a new destination. A new member may want to modify the plan to align with their own thoughts.

   When modifications to the plan are contemplated, a 3PM Leader will need to determine how this will affect the journey already in progress. A client considering a change to a plan often asks if that change is possible, and my response has always been: Anything can be done, it just depends on how much money you want to spend. Maybe the client doesn't like pretzels and would rather have Doritos. If we haven't bought the snack, there may be no change to cost; however, if the pretzels have been purchased, there will be a cost to buy the new snack. When a change in direction is asked for make sure to convey possible cost savings or additions.

Road trips should be fun and everyone on the journey has something great to offer. Having a road- tripper change mid road trip should only be a bump in the road. That bump doesn't need to be jaw jarring if the newly added member has been onboarded properly. When a 3PM Leader pursues these four points, I assure you that any team member transition will be much smoother. This roadmap may not avoid all the bumps, but it will certainly make it easier for you to grab the wheel and steer your project in the right direction. Enjoy your journey… and please, pass the pretzel sticks!

Managing the Process of the Plan

Once you have established a plan, that plan must be managed. But how do you manage the process of following through with a plan? Without team or collective understandings, success will mean something different for everyone. It will be a team in a tug-o-war contest with everyone pulling in a different direction. The first step in managing the process of planning is, after having and disseminating the plan, to make sure everyone is on the same team, pulling in the same direction. This is best accomplished during the team kick-off meeting where project information is shared and explained with a check for understanding. This is also a suitable time to ask your teammates what they would like to do or accomplish on the project.

As the plan is being executed, a great 3PM Leader will continuously monitor, anticipate, and respond to situations that require the plan to evolve and change. Managing the process of the plan also requires that you anticipate blind spots. Blind spots are prevalent on projects just like they are with your car. Things pop up seemingly out of nowhere. It takes experience and wisdom to anticipate, identify, and respond to blind spots. It is another Jedi power.

Quite often in my career, I anticipated and negated challenges or blind spots that I had encountered on similar project types. As an example, every new building project requires a local multi-step approval process. Because I have experience and knowledge that these approval processes can be complex and take months, I make these key issues and mitigate the blind spots that might happen here. Think of a blind spot like this: you are planning that family road trip in the family roadster, but you haven't done any maintenance on the vehicle for years. Without forethought, you can expect things to go wrong, to break. How will you handle the obstacles that are to come? Think of what preventative maintenance should be performed prior to departing on the road trip. Have a plan on how you will adjust your schedule if something goes wrong. Build contingencies into the project plan.

Identifying blind spots also requires a bit of listening to your inner voice. You may have a feeling in your gut that something seems off, or that something might go wrong with the present direction and will need to be addressed at some point. It is a 3PM Leader's superpower to recognize issues around the corner and go with their gut.

Being able to manage the process requires a 3PM Leader to have the ability to see things, recognize things no one else can see or imagine. It's like being a great chess player. I liken it to the quote by the world-renowned chess champion Bobby Fischer—"Tactics flow from a superior position." A great 3PM Leader, through a project plan, anticipates, calculates, and executes to stay in a place where they are always ahead and leading and never at a disadvantage.

As a chess player must anticipate the opponent's next move, so must a 3PM Leader anticipate next steps in a project plan and the next steps of their project team members. We must ensure that our teammates are following the project plan, staying on schedule with the work product, and maintaining the expected quality of the product. We need to be able to see where challenges may arise in the future through review and intimate familiarity with what it is our team is doing. By doing these things, we can stay ahead of surprises.

Feed Me, Seymour!

"Feed me, Seymour, feed me all night long. 'Cause if you feed me, Seymour, I can grow up big and strong!" Like Audrey II, from the blockbuster "Little Shop of Horrors" (the mysterious plant that looks like a Venus fly trap and avocado collided) asking to be fed, we also ask to be fed. Only we are asking for feedback, not blood. We are hungry for feedback that will help us grow big and strong. Feedback that will help us improve who we are and what we do. Feedback can also help in managing the process of the plan.

Feedback in terms of team members can help keep the team moving in the right direction and produce a product that will meet expectations. Feedback comes in several forms:

positive, negative, and neutral. Positive feedback reinforces behaviors we see as good. It is complimenting or recognizing someone for an action or work that has resulted in a positive outcome, experience, or product. Negative feedback points out behaviors, actions or processes we see as detrimental and needing adjustment, change, or correction. Neutral feedback includes general statements of observation. Real-time feedback enables a quick and immediate response to an issue that may be affecting a positive outcome. No matter the feedback, it must be constructive, and it must also be acknowledged and then addressed.

During a project, when a project plan is being executed, providing and receiving real-time feedback helps team members grow, get stronger, and improve what they do. I incorporated feedback into all my projects as part of the process. This can be a survey sent out to the client at milestones along the way. During kick-off meetings, I let the client know that we would be sending out surveys asking for feedback, and that I would be responding to every survey returned. Feedback questions to the client may include things like whether the team is meeting expectations, whether the team is listening to client input and responding to it, and whether the client feels the team is keeping them informed. Getting feedback from the client while the project is ongoing allows the team to adjust where needed to better meet the client's expectations. By doing this—asking for feedback and then addressing issues—an open and trusting relationship is built.

I once received feedback on a client survey indicating they felt we were not listening to their desires. I immediately sent out an email letting the client know that I had received their complaints and that I would like to have a conversation so we could mutually agree on how best to move forward and address their concern. When meeting with the client, the tone was of curiosity. I was there to discover the root of the concern and decide how best to address it. At the end of the meeting, I thanked them for the feedback, I outlined our agreed-upon solution, and then I implemented the solution. This situation and my response helped our team grow and get better at working with and listening to this client.

A 3PM Leader receives and acts on feedback given by teammates. Asking your team to provide feedback and then addressing it builds trust and respect. Receiving real-time feedback from your team and then responding requires you to be open and humble so you can quickly adjust or adapt to what is being pointed out. I received feedback from my team that the project schedule I put together was complicated and they were having a hard time following it. I took that feedback to heart and looked for another way to convey the information so that the team could better understand. This showed me that even though I could understand the schedule, others may need a different format to understand. Because I asked for feedback, listened, and acted, I was a better project manager and leader.

The 3PM Leader provides feedback to teammates. When expectations have been clearly communicated, but are not being met, this is a good time to provide redirecting feedback. A written plan outlining actions to be taken to meet expectations should be mutually created and agreed upon. The plan should also include a timeline for follow-up to ensure adherence to the plan. This is a great opportunity for mentoring and be a teaching moment.

When expectations are being met or exceeded the team members should receive that feedback as well. Point out what you appreciate, the positive action taken or the effort being applied. This feedback helps reinforce the attitude, behavior or actions you would like maintained, repeated or duplicated by others.

A 3PM Leader is also open to receiving feedback during the process. This feedback may come from the client or your internal team members. We need to be nimble in our role and adjust quickly to feedback provided if change is required. In this way, feedback is not relegated to after the fact and will help you stay on course and complete the journey successfully while meeting or—better yet—exceeding expectations.

CHAPTER 5

VALUING PEOPLE

Organization Dynamics

"I'm giving my two weeks' notice. I'm leaving for another opportunity." I often heard this as people I worked with looked for and found other positions and were leaving my company. Throughout my career, I managed and led people and teams. I saw people come and go from organizations looking for something they didn't seem to have at their current job, be it money, responsibility, career advancement opportunities, better work environment, you name it. When people left my organization, I felt sad for me and the organization, but happy that this person had decided to take a leap of faith and seek what they felt was right for them.

I have often said that everyone is replaceable, which I still believe to be true. When a person vacates a position at a company and interviews for the position occur, eventually, a new employee is placed into the existing role. Is the company the same? Will the product be the same? Will the environment be the same? The answer to each is no. And "no" doesn't mean it's better or worse, it just means it's different. Everyone in an organization brings skills, ethics, knowledge, and character. When a person leaves an organization and is replaced by another, it's important to understand that things will be different. The dynamics of the company and team will change. No one really fills the shoes of another. Positions are replaced by new employees, and the new person will add their own flavor to the firm.

My wife, daughter, and I went to dinner with some friends during the holiday season at a rustic restaurant with the feel of the lodge from the movie *White Christmas*—tall ceilings, large stone fireplaces, all the elements of a well-appointed log cabin. The aroma of a wood fire and gourmet food floated throughout the restaurant. After the meal, my daughter and I decided to split some dessert. We ordered a decadent double chocolate brownie with ice cream—yum! When the brownie came, both my daughter and I took a forkful and after a curious moment, we looked at each other as if to agree that this brownie was missing something. It looked exactly like the brownie we expected based on the menu description, but the texture and taste were different from what we thought it should be. Then it struck me: this was a gluten-free brownie. It was still a brownie, but the ingredients were different, and an ingredient had been substituted that changed it from what we typically tasted and expected.

Changing a person in a company is a very similar experience to an ingredient in a gluten-free brownie. It's still a brownie, it's called a brownie, it looks like a brownie, but something has changed to give it a different flavor, a different character. The change in ingredients is not good or bad from a taste standpoint, just different. People coming and going from organizations and your teams are like that brownie. Your organization or team is still doing what it is meant to do, but the ingredients are different.

As managers and leaders of people, we need to understand the dynamics of our teams and the people within them. Everyone brings something different to a team that affects the team dynamics. As people come and go, the make-up and chemistry will change, and it's your responsibility to understand how that change might affect the flavor, the character of your team.

Everyone on your team fits into a category ranging from those who will do anything to help the team and those that do enough just to squeak by. You have experts in their role and field and others who strive to be that person. You will have high energy, self-motivated team members eager to learn and others who will let opportunities go by with lack of effort and motivation. Each person, regardless of where they are in the spectrum of these categories, can be great contributors to a team—the opposite is also true. As a 3PM Leader, you will develop a sixth sense to identify these people on your team and ensure that you have a well-balanced team.

Image your full team working like a well-oiled machine; everything is going seamlessly, and then the person who has the most experience and knowledge leaves the team. This is the person the rest of the team relies on for technical direction. When that person leaves, the project manager will need to replace that role with a similar person, or the team will flounder trying to figure out the technical aspects of the project. If the 3PM Leader has not been paying attention to what each team member has been contributing, they may bring on the wrong person to fill that role.

Through years of experience working with many types of people and personalities, your sense of team make-up becomes keener. If you lack years of experience, you will need to carefully analyze personalities, skills, and motivational factors to advance your team intuition skills.

Every Person Has a Story

Everyone has professional and personal struggles that sometimes are visible, but most of the time are invisible. We are not a great society of sharers when it comes to personal struggles; acknowledging our daunting challenges to others can be seen as weakness. We see it every day. We see the façade people present when we ask in passing, "How you doing?" The expected reply is, "Pretty good. How 'bout you?" But this is a generic, numbing, and often fraudulent answer. We don't know truly how anyone is doing. Perhaps the person was just diagnosed with cancer and is struggling with what it all means. Maybe there are issues between siblings that are tearing the family apart. We all keep a stiff upper lip and present a stoic presence to the world. Being able to recognize when something is wrong, as a project manager, requires a keen sensibility and attentiveness, and responding in a compassionate way is essential.

A good leader sees and appreciates every person, meeting them where they are in the moment, and responding with care. The things happening—one's story being written—do affect that person's mindset which will also affect their work. When a person is going through a life-changing event, their focus on work also changes. When we lose focus on our work, mistakes happen, quality goes down, and overall engagement decreases. When you recognize these signs, you will be able to empathize with that person and adjust your team accordingly. In the end, you will become a better, more empathetic person and leader for having seen, understood, and responded. When you know your teammates and genuinely care for them, you will develop a sixth sense to detect subtle changes alerting you when a team member needs attention and support. A story in the Bible states it best:

"I am the good shepherd, who is willing to die for the sheep. When the hired man, who is not a shepherd and does not own the sheep, sees a wolf coming, he leaves the sheep and runs away; so the wolf snatches the sheep and scatters them. The hired man runs away because he is only a hired man and does not care about the sheep. I am the good shepherd. As the Father knows me and I know the Father, in the same way I know my sheep and they know me. And I am willing to die for them," (John 10:11-15 [GNT]). A good leader is like a good shepherd. They know their team and their team knows them. They know and care for each other. They put each other first.

Three years after Dawn and I were married, we had our first child—a boy, Bradley. We seemed to have won life's lottery. We both had successful careers in our chosen fields. We were both progressing in our careers and were given the opportunity for more and more responsibility. Dawn worked as a Registered Nurse in a cardiac department at a major hospital, while I found success within a renowned architectural firm. We were doing the things we wanted to do and what we went to college for. We moved from an apartment prior to having our baby and bought our first home to make our own. We were surrounded by loving and supportive family and friends. And then, we were blessed with a beautiful baby boy. Our young family cherished the many first-year moments like so many families do as they welcome a new baby into the family. We were shaping up to be the quintessential family.

Sixteen months after our baby boy was born, I had a medical appointment. It was a standard checkup, only the doctor discovered a lump on one of my testicles. He immediately sent me to get an MRI. It's funny, but I don't really remember getting the call from the doctor telling me I had cancer and that I needed to have surgery as soon as possible. It was all a blur. When you hear that you have cancer, your thoughts immediately go to: *Am I going to die?* Or at least mine did. Was I going to leave my wife alone to raise our son? Would I live to complete my personal vision plan? Cancer was going to kill me, I thought, and I would be leaving my wife and sixteen-month-old son respectively husbandless and fatherless. It seemed all my attention went from things outside my family, like work, to everything about my family. I do, however, vividly remember calling work and talking to my leader, telling him I had cancer and wouldn't be able to travel out of state to a job meeting I was scheduled to attend in just a few days. We spoke for a bit, problem-solving this situation, discussing the meeting particulars, what was to be covered, who else might be able to go in my place, and how we could transfer my airplane ticket to someone else. We even discussed when I might be back to work. I can picture the little cubicle at the clinic where I made the phone call—it was on a landline because cell phones were non-existent.

Looking back, I had my priorities out of order up until the word *cancer*. I didn't know if I was going to live or die, and if I did live, what that would look like moving forward and what my life expectancy would be. Dawn and I had always talked about having two children: a boy and girl. That was our definition of the perfect family. Would having a second child even be possible after the surgery and the radiation treatment to follow? Might there be more cancer in my body as yet undiscovered? Those who have been told they have cancer can relate to all these questions of future unknowns that permeate their thoughts. We often hear, "It's the *not knowing* that is the hardest," and I concur. My whole life changed in an instant, and I was worried about work. How crazy is that?

My leader did show compassion, but looking back, I see their priorities were out of order. Some of the questions being asked of me could have been answered by others. Some of the tasks I did after the diagnosis could have been done by other teammates. My leader should have told me to take care of myself and family and they would take care of everything else. None of this conversation felt right to me and I always thought if a conversation like this ever happened when I was in a leadership position, I would try to absorb the shock and show more care in handling the situation. I would not let work enter the conversation but would ask how I could help them and their family. After all, family should be the priority.

I never really heard of testicular cancer before my diagnosis, and I had no idea of the long-term prognosis. I caught it early and have been cancer free for decades now. Maybe because I didn't know how to talk about it or was somehow embarrassed to talk about it, or maybe because I didn't want people to see me in the shadow of what cancer can imply, but I did not tell many people. I think even close friends today reading this book will be surprised to learn this news. Having cancer can put a label on you, put you in the spotlight, like being labeled by the color of your skin or your religious beliefs, and I didn't want to be labeled. So, I kept the news to a very small circle of family and friends. Two years after my diagnosis, my wife and I were blessed with our second child – a girl, Kaytlyn.

Having cancer, in a strange sense, may have saved my life by helping me get my priorities in order. Family does come first, and work should always be second—always, period. It also helped me realize that probably everyone is going through some personal struggle they conceal from view. Why they do or don't share is personal.

During my years of leading teams, I have watched team members deal with life-changing events, both good and not-so-good. My life experience of having cancer, I believe, has helped me be more empathetic towards my coworkers' life-changing events. Having cancer gets you laser-focused on your life in figuring out how you are going to deal with the disease. Everything else fades out of thought and becomes more of a distraction. Staying engaged at work with all of this in your head, for me, was very difficult, and I am certain others feel the same.

I had a coworker once tell me that they were going to miss their daughter's event because a client request needed to be addressed. I asked what needed to be done. After a brief conversation, I told this person to leave and go to his daughter's event; that we, his team, would get the request out to the client for him. I told him that family is more important. I think sometimes putting family first, in our current society, has a false indication of weakness or non-committal attitude. I believe the opposite is true. When your basic needs are met, you are more likely to be all in for your team and your work.

Everyone has a story they may be writing in silence, and the story being written will affect their work. It is up to leaders to take the burden off their shoulders and help with the heavy lifting of life's obstacles. A good leader, a good shepherd, will be able to sense when something is off in a teammate. There is almost an innate parental instinct that one gets when sensing these things. Be mindful of such occurrences and take up the line. Are there things you can do to help ease the burden and support the person and their family? Every person has a story, written or unwritten, for us to read or uncover. A great 3PM Leader will discover people's stories and support them.

Your Team Members Are Your People

Being a 3PM Leader means truly caring for your team, client, and work. Most think project managers just tell people what to do and when to do it. However, this is not my definition. I view project management as managing projects, people, and a process by providing guidance, wisdom, and compassion. Your team does most of the actual work, and you help to manage that work. You are working for your team, not the other way around. A 3PM Leader, when talking to their team members, is humbled to realize how they impact lives and careers.

Empathy must be genuine, active, and tangible. Just because I am telling you to be caring, and you say you are caring, doesn't mean you *truly* care. To gauge empathy, I challenge you to create a list of how you have cared for your team or client recently. How have you proactively shown empathy for others? Be mindful of what is happening in your teams' personal lives and try to ease their burden at work. Your teammates will make many sacrifices for their work and their job. Most of those sacrifices will be taken at the expense of their family. How will you recognize those sacrifices? How will you help promote setting work aside when family is needed first?

Caring for your team, really caring for your team, is not just saying the words—it's your actions that show you care. Give credit to your team in a genuine way; after all, they are the ones doing most if not all the work. I have seen leaders give credit to others for something they didn't do and everyone in the room knew it. This is not genuine, and it shows that this person is not really connected to their team. Give credit where credit is due, but don't give credit to others just to boost their self-esteem or yours. Give it genuinely, from a sense of deep appreciation.

Are you a self-promotor or do you promote your team and what they accomplished? Do you start most of your conversations with "I did this" or "I created this"? Indeed, sometimes you are the person who did these things, however, there are times when you may be leading a team where you promote yourself rather than the team who did the toughest work. When managing teams, promoting the team rather than yourself will develop respect and trust that you will give credit where it is due. It shows humility and true servant-leadership.

Years ago, I was at a seminar where this topic was being discussed. Someone mentioned they recognize the sacrifice that the family, the spouse and kids made, so their spouse, mom or dad, could stay late and work or go on a business trip. Think about the hand-off of responsibility between spouses when one has to spend more time at work or go out of town on a business trip. The drop-offs and pick-ups at school and day care, the chauffeuring to practices and the cheffing of meal preparation. Even if no children are involved, there is still sacrifice that occurs by the spouse in losing time together and taking responsibility for daily tasks.

Even a simple note to the team member's spouse thanking them for their support and the time they sacrificed is meaningful. It was easy to relate this to my own life. I saw the sacrifice my family made so I could be all-in in terms of my career.

Because of this seminar, I started sending out thank you notes to my teammates' spouses thanking them for supporting their loved ones in their careers and helping them to fulfill project requirements. It was a small gesture of thanks. Years after these notes were sent, I still have spouses of co-workers saying how much those notes meant to them.

I started paying more attention to the sacrifices and real-life struggles my teammates made and were going through. My personal calendar was filled with anniversaries, dates of happy events like marriages, births, and birthdays. My calendar also filled with anniversaries of the painful nature like miscarriages, deaths of family members, and other traumatic events. All these calendar entries, when they came up, reminded me what each person experienced and sacrificed during this period and that I needed to be sensitive, especially to workloads. A true 3PM leader must be aware and give space for teammates to celebrate, mourn, process, and reflect. How you respond to personal events will differ based on the relationship you have with the individual, however, if you have shown compassion and empathy and you have showed caring in the past, you have built a personal relationship enough to respond in a supportive and loving way.

Another part of people management is building lasting relationships. Relationships and friendships take time to develop. Honesty and trust are key components to building relationships. View it as an investment that gives you nothing back. If you give to a relationship or friendship, your expectation should be to get nothing in return. The return is intrinsic, automatic. True long-lasting relationships and friendships will last through time if this invisible exchange of investment is freely given. It's when it is not freely given that these relationships do not last, and you fall away. Think about your longest and deepest friendship. I imagine if that person asked you for a favor, you would drop everything to help and vice versa. Developing meaningful relationships is its own reward.

In life, it's everyone's responsibility to help others. We improve this world by caring, sharing our knowledge, our expertise, and our wisdom so others can learn and become better. Leaders must not be afraid for others to succeed. In fact, I contend that it is a leader's responsibility, part of their mission, to help others succeed. By helping, you prove that you care. The term "servant-leader" has been a buzz word for a while. A servant-leader is someone who leads their team by serving them and helping them to be the best version of themselves. Look for ways to help your team and each member succeed in what they are doing, in their work and in their life.

Be Your Team's Knight in Shining Armor

Your armor is what people see in you, what you project outwardly, and what reflection you give back to your team members about themselves. Your armor is hammered out, kept smooth and polished, by adherence to your values and beliefs. It is embellished with trust, kindness, compassion, and empathy. Our armor starts out bright and shiny—a pristine coat of arms, one we are proud of and are happy when others take notice. When we deviate from who we are, what we believe, and our values, we get a dent or tarnish in this armor. The severity of the dent or tarnish is dependent on the degree of deviation from our personal compass. These deviations deteriorate how your team thinks of you. Rather than a bright and shiny leader, one they are proud of and have respect for, you become the opposite.

Prior to getting married, my wife and I purchased a 1971 Volkswagen Beetle convertible from a car lot— and I am being generous in calling it a car lot. This lot was one step away from a junkyard. I had learned how to drive a manual transmission, a stick shift, on our family's Beetle; these cars had a special place in my heart. This car would need a lot of work after we towed it home. You read that right—we had to tow it home, as it was undrivable. Once pristine when it rolled off the production line in Germany, this car had been without a scratch, dent, or blemish. I'm certain it was carefully driven at first, parked a mile away from the grocery cart corrals. People noticed the shiny, new car. In time, it got its first dent. The owner started not caring as much for it and parked ever-so-close to that cart corral. Over the years, the car lost its luster as the many dents, rust spots, and lost hub caps made the car less appealing. Eventually, with many miles and a lack of maintenance, the car was kicked aside and scrapped.

Every car starts out as a shiny, smooth, perfectly clean automobile complete with that new car smell. That's us when we start out in a career, especially as project managers. We are ready for the journey ahead with all our brights spots and perfect shine. We have a glow of excitement and newness. As we continue, we try to stay true to our values and beliefs, to keep that new car shine without a ding or rust spot. Eventually we will do something that compromises who we are or what we do and, all of a sudden, we have a small dent, a nick in the paint. We have a chink in our personal armor.

After we towed the car home we started a disassembly process, labeling every part and taking notes as to how we had taken it apart. We purchased new parts to replace the dented and rusted pieces. We reupholstered the seats and readied the car for new paint. After thirty years of sitting in our garage in an unfinished state, my wife and I had to make the decision—do we give up on the undrivable car or do we restore it? We chose to bring it back to life. Over the next two years, we worked to restore it to drivable condition. The car was a piece of history, a story that needed to be saved and retold. It was loaded into a box trailer and taken to a local restoration shop where it would go through a major transformation before it was brought back home to us on a flatbed tow truck. My wife and I then took the next year to complete the restoration. It is hard to describe the pride and sense of accomplishment felt as my wife and I (along with some friends standing by with fire extinguishers) started the engine. We smiled a smile of satisfaction as we drove down the driveway. We had rebuilt, rewritten, and reinvented the once beloved Beetle convertible to its former glory. It took time to make it new again. It's so fun now driving our Ferrari-red VW Beetle convertible down the street with people turning their heads to admire it. The removal of the dents and rust, the complete restoration, is a joy for my wife, myself, and all those who get to see it.

If you allow yourself or others to dent your mission, beliefs, or values, over time you will have so many dents that you might not be recognizable, just like that old Volkswagen we purchased. We can avoid these dents and blemishes by staying true to our beliefs and values, however, if we do end up with a few dings, we should not see all has hopeless. We, too, can reinvent ourselves if we become riddled with dents and blemishes. It will take time. If we have lost the respect, trust, and reliability of our team through our actions, we can slowly gain it back by advocating for our team based on our beliefs and values.

Start with who you are and what you believe, and you will be the sentinel for your team. It's a 3PM Leader's responsibility to be their team's biggest advocate, to stand up for them, to be a shield which will deflect or absorb stresses or pressure being applied to a team from outside forces. Those pressures can come from your leader, your client, and even you! Through your actions of advocacy, you will construct a foundation of trust, reliability, camaraderie, and respect.

I have been forced to carry the beliefs of others even when in conflict with my own. As one builds what some call social equity, the ability to be forthright during difficult situations is imperative. Telling your leader or client that what they are asking for is going to hurt the team and have an adverse effect rather than an intended positive one is difficult. However difficult it may seem, when we stand up for our team using our values and beliefs as guideposts, we will have an easier time of it. We must be the shield, our team's biggest advocate, regardless of the situation.

Situations are only difficult if we allow them to be, if we go against what we believe in attempting to address them. If we are honest with ourselves, these conversations should be able to flow easily. That's not to say that they won't be uncomfortable, however, receiving uncomfortable words from someone who is caring, humble, and authentic can be a learning and mentoring experience even for a leader.

Sometimes situations arise where you are asked to convey information to your team that you feel may not be appropriate. You may be asked or told to do something that goes against your beliefs. You may be asking an already overworked team to work more—to put in extra hours when they are already doing it. You may be asked to tell someone that they are not meeting a work utilization number that is meaningless. In cases such as these, where our leaders are telling us to communicate a message that we do not believe to be true, we must stand up and be advocates for our teammates. If we don't stand by what we believe to be true, if we abandon our values and beliefs, our team will see it and we will get a chink, a small dent, in our armor. Our team will lose that trust, reliability, camaraderie, and respect we tried so hard to build.

Your Clients Are People, Too

I have had the privilege to work with some amazing people as clients. I'm often asked what my favorite project was and why. My favorite projects have been those where our entire team, including the client, had fun doing the project and it was one we could all be proud of. Within these projects was camaraderie among the team members and mutual respect, appreciation, and understanding of the expertise each member brought to the team. We valued each other's opinions, and we sought to find the best outcome for all participants in the process. These are the projects and clients everyone wants to work with, where good relationships and friendships are made, and there is positive synergy in the air.

That's not to say there weren't tough conversations or disagreements along the way, but there was always cordiality, honesty, and respect. Once the issues were resolved, we moved on from it and didn't hold it as a bargaining chip. I'm going to call these good clients.

Partnering with good clients is easy when you consider it just that: a partnership where both parties desire the same goal. Establishing this attitude and working from there allows for a smoother process from the start. Such clients are friendly, collaborative, understanding and open, respectful, humble, and lighthearted. These are clients who want and appreciate the expertise you bring to the process; after all, it's why they hired you! I have had clients say they "trust the process," which essentially means they recognize there is a process; they are willing to walk into the unknown where some parts may seem confusing because they trust your leadership and expertise.

Now, we don't get these types of clients all the time; in fact, sometimes we get the opposite type of clients. You might inherit a client you just don't connect with or feel you cannot work with. Finding common ground is difficult and takes effort and time. These clients, too, hired you for your expertise, therefore, we must find a way to connect and provide exceptional service to them as well. Sometimes, it takes all your people skills to work with a not-so-good client, and they can never know that this is how you've categorized them or that you've categorized them at all.

To understand your client, you must understand their personality. A DISC analysis will provide ideas or strategies on how best to work and communicate with them. DISC is an acronym that stands for the four main personality profiles described in the DISC model: (D)ominance, (I)nfluence, (S)teadiness and (C)onscientiousness.

- People with D personalities tend to be confident and place an emphasis on accomplishing bottom-line results.
- People with I personalities tend to be more open and place an emphasis on relationships and influencing or persuading others.

- People with S personalities tend to be dependable and place an emphasis on cooperation and sincerity.
- People with C personalities tend to place an emphasis on quality, accuracy, expertise, and competency.

DISC is just one of many personality tests available, including the 16 Personalities test; use the one that best suits you. I worked with a construction firm who would lead a DISC assessment at the project kickoff meeting. It was a great way for the entire team to learn more about each other and have a bit of fun in the process.

Understanding who I am and who others are helps communication. If I'm working with a D – Dominance personality, I know they don't want me to take time to give them all the details that I worked through; they just want the answer. Knowing this will help me get right to the point and not bore them with what may really excite me. Understanding personality types and strategies on how to deal with those who are different from you will improve your effectiveness as a 3PM Leader.

I have had the opportunity to work with all kinds of clients—public and private; sole ownerships; Fortune 500 companies; amiable and forceful; decisive and indecisive; kind and not-so-kind, collaborative and obstructionist. You get the picture. Of these different types of clients, each one required different skills to manage and lead. Each person brings value to a project and team, however we, as project managers, are responsible for bringing out the best in each person.

Getting to know who your client is both from a contractual standpoint and personality standpoint will help you navigate decision-making and help smooth out rough spots that inevitably surface. There are always rough spots, but as author and minister Max Lucado so aptly quoted, "Conflict is inevitable; combat is optional." I have discovered that to have a cohesive team, one that works together well, one that can marinate into a wonderful, blended team, more than anything else, it's about personal connections.

CHAPTER 6

MANAGING THE CLIENT PARTNERSHIP

Know Your Client

A technical definition for client is the person or entity who engages your professional advice or services. Clients are the ones who are paying you for your services. They most likely signed your contract. In my case, most of my clients were school districts, although the board of education was the actual client. The board of education president typically signed our contracts, but they were not the person making daily decisions about the project; decisions were left to an administrative leader or a core team of leaders.

I have had clients where a team of people made the decisions collectively and with consensus. This works if there is one person on the team responsible for ensuring that a decision is made. This person facilitates a process with the client team in decision-making. This person should be identified in the contract as the decision-maker.

Yet after we understand the difference between the client and decision makers from a technical perspective, we need to know each as a person. We must understand what they are passionate about, what their hot buttons are, so we can best meet their needs and expectations.

Since my work involved working with school districts and their boards, I met and interacted with dozens of school board members who ultimately were my clients. While working with school board members, patterns in personalities emerged. Knowing what they cared about and why they were on the board helped me better manage all the different personalities. As I sat in board meetings, I would try to figure what category each member fit into. People fell into seven categories I created. In my experience, most clients fall into one of these categories:

1. The Uniter. This person brings everyone to a consensus by negotiating ideas. They respectfully and thoughtfully present and listen to ideas and opinions in a non-threatening way. This person will help the entire group accept new ideas or stand firm on non-negotiables.

2. Agenda Holder. This person has one item they feel strongly about, and they will be a champion for that. Leverage that one thing they champion to keep them engaged.

3. The Obstructionist. This person is upset about one thing and will go in the opposite direction of the board just because they can. Work to understand the one thing and see if there is a way to address it so you can soften their stance.

4. Back Seater. This person thought it would be cool to have an air of prestige associated with being elected to

the school board but has no real interest. Engage this person with conversation and eye contact about issues and ask how you can help them better understand what is being presented.

5. The Analyzer. This person will ask all the tough questions and push to have data to back up their decision or claim. Work to get this person the information they are asking for even though you may think it's exhaustive. You will need to anticipate and stay ahead of the questions to come.

6. The Oblivious. This person lacks the ability to understand complex issues being discussed and seems to be confused most of the time. Set time aside outside of meetings to work with them to better understand where the confusion lies and clear it up.

7. Lone Cowboy. This person emphatically pushes their ideas and opinions; they want what they want. They believe that their ideas are the best and will fight tooth and nail to ensure that direction is taken. Ensure that you are considering their ideas and look for "and" rather than "but" solutions. "Interesting idea, *and*..." not "interesting idea, *but*..." Not every idea is a good idea, but it is our job as project managers and leaders to consider all options.

Once you decide how you will determine client personality types (using the resources or tools mentioned in the previous section or ones of your choice), you must then adjust your approach to best accommodate each. Understanding where people are coming from, who they are, and what motivates them will help you better negotiate the process of managing and leading them. It will help you better communicate with them. It may also give you strategies on how best to approach crucial conversations.

The basis for attempting to work well and communicate with each of these personality types is to look for the good in people (there IS good in everyone) and understand where they are coming from. Project managers must also remember to maintain control of their emotions to better manage others' emotions. Start from the point of view that the person you are working with is a good person and wants to do what is right, even if what they think is right doesn't mesh with your idea. Assume they believe they are right for the right reasons—always.

I'm an optimist and try to find the good in everyone, to understand views opposing my own, however, reality takes priority. I have had some clients who did not fit my "good client" definition, and I had to flex my personality style, communication style, harden my already tough skin, and seek advice from others. When you are working with a not-so-good client, it is important to understand your limits and to adhere to who you are and what you believe. Do not stray from who you are—stand tall with your morals, values, and beliefs. Considering that a project can last for years, and you will be working closely with the client for that period, I believe developing a good partnership that epitomizes all the attributes that make a good client partnership is essential. It's hard work, but you can get there.

Some clients have unreasonable expectations related to services, schedules, and costs because each of these is likely far different from what they were just a decade ago. Most often, misunderstanding is at the root of unrealistic expectations. Impatience and an unclear understanding of how long a project takes is another point of potential contention. Society in general is at a point where we want immediate satisfaction, and we don't want to wait; we demand instant gratification. While we may grow impatient waiting in the drive-thru line or waiting on food to be delivered to our doors, most professional services are not available instantaneously. Helping a client understand the complete process and a realistic timeframe at the onset will help ensure success for the project team. Knowing how best to communicate this process requires an understanding of who your client is.

Poor Behavior

Let's have a difficult conversation. Throughout your professional career, heck even in your day-to-day life, you may deal with people you'd rather not be working with. Yes, there are good clients and bad clients, ones who are a dream to work for and others who, well, just behave poorly. However, you will have to deal with them the same as all the rest of your team with respect, dignity, and humility. Everyone deserves the same level of respect even if it is not reciprocated. Don't let someone else's bad behavior affect your behavior. My wife has a saying—"Kill them with kindness"—meaning those who treat others poorly seem to get upset when the person receiving the poor treatment responds with positivity and kindness. You can only control yourself—you cannot control other people—and you can only change yourself, so don't try to change others.

An associate of mine was attending a meeting in my stead. It was a crucial presentation of a facilities report, which gives an overview of the condition of a building or buildings and its systems, like electrical and plumbing. This report had six buildings listed and was the size of a metro phonebook. The presentation is a broad overview of the report with all the details saved in the report.

My associate had done much of the leg work investigating the condition of each building. They had also worked closely with engineers to evaluate electrical, plumbing, and mechanical systems. They knew the information inside and out. The presentation was complex in that it involved multiple schools' condition reports outlining areas for needed repairs. After over thirty minutes of presenting the report, one board member asked a very detailed question and wanted to know where specific information was in the two-inch-thick binder. My associate told her where the information was and, in response, the board member indicated that he didn't really care where the information was, only that my associate knew where the information was. Clearly, this board member was trying to trip up my associate just to make them look bad. This board member was showing a lack of respect and professionalism—they were behaving poorly.

In this situation, my associate took the question and responded professionally and with respect knowing this person was trying to trip them up. This would not be the last time this board member would behave poorly; however, we could now predict some of the behavior which allowed us to better be prepared. We could anticipate questions that might come up and mentally prepare ourselves for this person knowing what their motivation might be. We wanted to be professional and respectful even if it was not returned.

When working with a client, it is good to set boundaries of acceptable behavior. We often say to clients, "You can call me anytime," but we don't really mean it. Even if we don't voice it, there are boundaries separating work and personal life. Time is one of those implied boundaries. I think most would agree that a client calling your cell phone before 8 a.m. and after 5:00 p.m. or on a weekend or holiday is out of bounds unless you have explicitly had a conversation expanding your availability.

We had a client who was calling an associate at all hours of the day, regardless of the day of the week. These were not just quick phone calls either; they would last sometimes for an hour. This client did not respect personal boundaries and was behaving poorly. My associate, wanting to be respectful of our client, would take these calls but eventually had to have a conversation with the client setting boundaries as to when they would receive their phone calls or respond to emails.

It's always easier to work with someone who you get along with—those possessing attributes of a good client. It's harder to work with someone who embodies the opposite. It seems taboo to label or talk about bad clients, however, let's strategize how we can be successful or at least survive such clients.

A 3PM Leader will have a thorough understanding of the client, their personality, and their motivations. They will anticipate questions, behaviors and possible blind spots and be prepared to navigate through the rough waters when they arise; they will do all of this in a respectful manner.

The Grudge-Holder

In the Christmas movie, *A Christmas Story*, which takes place in in the 1940s, nine-year-old Ralphie, dreams of finding a "Red Ryder Carbine-action 200-shot Range Model Air Rifle" under his Christmas tree on Christmas morning. Much of the story takes place with Ralphie and his friends either walking to and from school or in the classroom. One day, while walking home from school, Ralphie, his good friend Flick, and his brother Randy came face-to-face with Scut Farkus and his crony, Grover Dill. Scut and Grover were both bullies who enjoyed tormenting the boys day after day as they walked home from school. Can you relate more to Ralphie or Scut Farkus?

When I was in elementary school, I had a very similar experience to Ralphie's. My story starts in winter at an elementary school playground with snowbanks as tall as the school itself that surrounded the entire playground. Somehow, I got on the wrong side of the school bully, let's call him Dirk. During recess on a gray midwinter's morning with a playground full of kids, Dirk was looking for me to inflict either emotional or physical harm, and I sought shelter on the back side of the towering snow piles created by the snowplow. I think this is where I learned to be stealthy and thought I would make a good spy. I would stick my head ever so slightly above the snow pile peaks to seek out Dirk's location and, like a spider clinging to a wall, I would move along the steep slope of the snowbank in the opposite direction. I was positive my pounding heart would reveal my location it was banging so hard inside my chest. Then, the bell rang! It was time to go back into school. The whole playground full of kids started to empty and I noticed that Dirk and his crony were staying back, looking past the kids to seek me out in the crowd. Somehow, I did get back into school and passed the bully gauntlet unharmed. My experience on that elementary school playground helped me build a chest of tools that help me cope and navigate situations like this. I saw bullies at a young age, and it was then that I started to figure out how to cope with them.

With some conflicts, it's hard to trace where it all started. A bump, a stare, an exchange of unpleasantries, or no reason at all. Encountering bullies can paralyze you and make you react in unreasonable ways; you may even become the bully. I'm not sure that they ever shake that feeling of wanting to inflict emotional or physical harm on others, and sometimes, as in the case of Dirk, it seems to be just for sport. In a professional setting, however, there is no place to hide, so you must hit bullies head-on, metaphorically speaking.

On several occasions I have experienced clients who held grudges that seemed to arise out of nothing. They degraded, insulted, mocked, disrespected, and disregarded others seemingly to elevate their own status or agenda. Having a bully on the team leads to dysfunction and high tension because the person lacks respect for others. Holding true to who you are is vitally important so that you don't get kicked around or steamrolled over. If you hold true to who you are, you can navigate this team dynamic, albeit your heart may race at times, and you might want to hide behind a pile of snow. Understanding how you react to these types of situations and having strategies to help mitigate reactions can help you deal with the bully.

A firm I worked for believed in surveying clients at milestones throughout the entire process of design and construction of a building so that we could address issues before they became insurmountable. A client consistently gave me low scores and provided comments that related to an issue that had occurred years prior (hence, the grudge). This person and I had conversations regarding the past issue, and they indicated they had gotten past it. However, they had not. Even after having several face-to-face meetings, the comments would still appear on surveys. At some point, you must stop allowing these types of people to undermine surveys, as they add no constructive feedback.

Knowing the type of person you are dealing with will help you place yourself in a place of acceptance of the situation. You cannot change other people, and in some cases, you can never please them. You can only change yourself. You may not be able to please them, however, you should always do what is right by that person.

I took the approach that I would listen to this person, seek how to incorporate their ideas and thoughts into the project and, if possible, seek ways to improve on their ideas. After all, they were the client, and I was designing a building for them. I tried to avoid confrontational approaches I knew would bring out the worst in this person; I would not stoop to their level. This doesn't mean that I gave into or accepted an ideology that didn't fit into my beliefs and values—quite the contrary. If you know who you are, you can be stronger in your approach and communication.

As a professional, you must know your limits when it comes to pushing your own ideas with a client. Yes, we must share our professional opinions and lead the client. However, if the client does not want or respect your professional opinions, you must move on and take their direction. This may sound like a defeatist attitude, however, if no professional ethics or laws are being broken, it is time to move on and push the process forward.

Kicking and Screaming: The Tantrum-Thrower

Once, I worked with a district that utilized a client-team approach. They had many people at the table with no one stepping forward to take leadership of making decisions or having the final word. It was a multiheaded client with a poorly defined leadership structure. Part of the project we were working on for them was to design a "world-class" athletic complex—"world-class" being an ambiguous term that did little in the way of defining expectations.

Like all legitimate projects, this one had a defined budget based on the agreed-upon scope of work. At some point in the process, the district wanted to add more scope without adding more money. That's like saying you want more toppings on your pizza but aren't willing to pay for them! This would never work, and something had to give.

We had a meeting about the athletic fields and did some puzzle play. Puzzle play is where we take small pieces of paper representing items such as a baseball field, a football field, tennis courts, etc. and start to lay out a site plan with all desired amenities. We place the pieces on a drawing of the entire site to see how they all will fit. This meeting included several people from the school district and me. Going into this meeting, I knew that there wasn't money for what the district wanted, and I knew working through this and prioritizing needs was going to be challenging based on previous experiences with the client and the lack of responsibility taken.

The district was trying to put ten acres of athletic fields onto a five-acre site. At one point in the meeting, one client-team member started pacing like a caged lion because things were not going their way. I tried to soothe the situation by providing options and speaking in a calming voice, which may have made the person even more furious as his tactics weren't bothering me. Suddenly, he became enraged and tossed his chair, yelling that he was not getting what he wanted. I was shocked! How could a leader, teacher, and person of authority act like this and treat others with such disrespect? I started wondering if a physical attack was imminent. The rest of the meeting is a blur, as I was more concerned about my wellbeing than the client's needs at that point.

After the meeting, I documented the conversation in the meeting minutes, minus the tossing of chair. I also made a mental note to myself that I would not meet with this person alone and I would try to work through other channels to present and get information from this person. No one should have to put up with others who are that disrespectful. I never received an apology from the person for the way they acted, nor did I expect one.

I thought about how I might better handle situations like this in the future or avoid them altogether. Upon reflection, I should have told this person right then and there that his behavior was not acceptable, and I should have ended the meeting to be continued at another time when we could talk and allow the situation to cool. I could have also approached one of the other client team leaders and asked for their assistance in managing the situation.

Being in the middle of a career prevented me from taking the actions I would take today, more experienced and wiser. No one should ever be afraid to leave a situation where they are feeling disrespected or fear for their safety.

Knocking People Down: When Clients Are the Bullies

Do for others what you want them to do for you – Matthew 7:12. This quote from the Bible is saying to us that we should emulate the respect, kindness, empathy, and compassion we are expecting in return from others.

Have you ever gotten something put in your lap and you think this is too good to be true? Most likely it is too good to be true. There are circumstances hidden to you that will be revealed as you move through the process. Being able to recognize this and going in with eyes wide open will help you navigate what may come.

Our firm was hired by a district whose superintendent interviewed only two or three firms. No one really knew the exact number of firms he interviewed because he was not forthcoming with this information. This is unusual because a school district is a public entity and there are typically policies outlining requirements for hiring consultants with an open and competitive process. This was the first red flag.

There was another firm that had been doing projects in the district for years, and the buildings and grounds director had a great relationship with them. The buildings and grounds director and I knew each other through other organizations we belonged to and events we attended. He made it clear from the beginning of this project that he would rather be working with his favorite firm, not ours. Another red flag.

All my projects start with a kick-off meeting which typi-cally includes the entire client's team and all those who would be involved in the project. This superintendent said he was the only one that needed to be at the kick-off meeting. He did, however, acquiesce when we scheduled team meetings where we would ultimately start to design the building and require input from many district leaders. A third red flag.

This superintendent ended up being a bully I had to deal with. Rather than building people up and relying on their expertise, he would knock them down and dismiss them. How many red flags did we have before this? I lost count.

This type of behavior led to others working behind the superintendent's back. It was a toxic environment where collaboration and openness were almost impossible and backroom deals were the order of the day. This led me to learn how to build bridges between conflicting personalities and agendas. It was like walking a high wire line; I felt like a Flying Wallenda. Every presentation, every meeting required me to balance adhering to the client's goals and what was ethical.

Throughout this entire project, everyone was walking on eggshells trying not to crack them for fear it would release an onslaught of verbal insults and bullying. Now you might be asking, why didn't I fire this client? Can a project manager move to fire a client? Absolutely! And, trust me, we held internal discussions about this. In the end, it came down to my firm needing the project, as it was at a time when the market was slow. So, I had to cope the best I could and make the project as successful as possible.

Working with clients like this is when it is critical to know who you are—your values and what you believe in. A strong moral compass will compel you to create and protect boundaries so you don't allow anything to degrade your reputation or tarnish the trust of your team. It is also important, especially when working with difficult clients, to keep clear and complete meeting minutes, as they document conversations and decisions made.

I recall a meeting where a decision needed to be made. At the time, the CEO said he didn't need to be involved in the process and that he didn't need to be part of the final decision. The research was done, a decision made, and a solution put in process. At a job meeting where we were discussing the implementation of the solution, the CEO jolted up from his notes and exclaimed that he was not aware of this and, with a raised voice, exclaimed his disapproval at me for not consulting with him. I reminded him of our previous conversation where he bowed out of this issue, which he denied. I pulled up the meeting minutes on my computer and read them. He denied what I read was true, but I held firm to the notes and documented decision and asked if he wanted us to revisit the issue so he could be involved. Keep in mind that this would have been an additional service since we would have already done the work based on his direction. Instead, he told us to move on and keep doing what we were doing.

It can be hard to stand up to someone like this and hold your moral ground but, when in the right, you must do so regardless of the consequences. If I had given in to bullish behavior, my character would have taken a dent from everyone at every meeting table. You must hold true to who you are and what you stand for; if you don't, your armor gets chinked.

Know When to Hold 'Em

All clients deserve our full arsenal of professionalism. We have control over how we interact with them. It is vital to understand who we are so that how we react in certain situations, especially challenging ones, suits our character and always presents our best.

Even if we think we know what people are going through, we really don't. Everyone responds differently to pressure, and it can be either a good, bad, or indifferent response. I had been working with this client for several years. We were in the throes of design, and I was looking for answers to questions that had been out to the client for a while. I decided to call and see if there was anything I could do to help move the decision-making process along. As our conversation began, I could tell the superintendent's voice—his tone and inflection—was off. He seemed distracted, and I asked if I should call back at a different time. I knew something was not right and now was not the best time to be asking for decisions or having a critical conversation.

When he responded that it was a good time to talk, however, I continued as if nothing were wrong. After only a few minutes into our discussion, I got blasted with a raised voice and uncharacteristic comments. We ended the conversation with my wondering what had just happened; I felt a bit wounded but was more concerned for my client and what had moved him to be someone I didn't recognize.

A few days later, I had an in-person meeting with this same superintendent. He apologized for his actions. He said he should have taken my offer to speak at a different time because only an hour prior to our conversation, he had found out that his teenage, unmarried daughter was pregnant. The news was unsettling to him, and he was in a state of shock and dismay.

This exchange was monumental for me in how I moved forward in leadership. I learned that it is ok to ask to continue a conversation at another time if there are distractions too large to overcome in the moment. I also learned that, as a leader, having the grace to acknowledge you made a mistake in how something was handled elevates your perception and doesn't degrade respect. It shows you are human and have a heart.

I still use this strategy today. If I can tell that someone is distracted to the point having a succinct conversation will not be possible, I ask if we should hold off and schedule a different time. In this case, it's ok to fold temporarily. Asking the question gives the other person an easy out to take a breath and recenter themselves. You are giving them permission to regroup and say, "Yes, now isn't a good time. Let's talk later."

CHAPTER 7

I LEARNED FROM THAT

The Story in Your Head

"Boy, I didn't see that coming!" This is something we often say to ourselves when an outcome doesn't match the story we consciously wrote in our minds. When a conflict arises, we start to troubleshoot possible scenarios and write a narrative, a story of what we think will happen, in our minds; in many cases, this is far from reality.

When I started my architectural career, I drew everything by hand. Yes, yes, it's hard to believe, but architectural drawings were not always done electronically. There was an art to hand-drawing and, as some wise architect once told me, "When you draw a line, you better know what it is." What he meant was when you draw a line, know what it represents. A line can be the edge of a wood stud, a piece of metal roof flashing, or a sprayed-on vapor barrier that is paper thin. If something changed on a paper drawing, the old was erased, the erasure shniblits (yes this is a real word in *my* dictionary) were brushed away, and a line representing the new was drawn. Hand-drawing took time, and it helped pace your thinking.

I came into architecture as CAD (Computer-Aided Design) was becoming more prevalent. With CAD, what a line represents still held true, but things were not necessarily erased, rather, they were stretched, dragged, moved, or rotated, which could and did lead to errors and misrepresentations on drawings. CAD drawing happened instantaneously. You clicked here and there and voila, a line was drawn. Sure, there was thought that went into that line, however, CAD could move faster than your brain was thinking.

I worked at a design-build firm for several years. A design-build firm has both architects and contractors, architects who design buildings and contractors who build those buildings. The thought is that this gives an owner one source, one company to contact, if there are any issues. It is touted as helping with coordination and ensuring the whole process will go more smoothly.

I was working with a national furniture retail company to build new and renovate existing buildings. One such renovation project was in Memphis, Tennessee, and as a young, upcoming architect, I thought it most excellent that I was traveling to do projects. When you are young, traveling for work elevates your self-esteem; it's like you've made the big time!

For this project, I had completed CAD documents for the renovation of an old, bankrupt department store into a new furniture store, and our construction team was on-site building. The renovation involved a complete gutting of the interior and the addition of a significant exterior entrance canopy built with three-foot diameter, ten-feet tall solid concrete columns, and a steel gable roof structure. The layout of this furniture store was consistent around the country for every store. A customer's experience started at the curb; they would walk under the entrance canopy, open the doors, and walk a few feet to a circular information desk that greeted every guest. The entrance was centered directly on the circular information desk. It would be the first thing a customer would see.

One day while working in the office, I received a call from our on-site construction superintendent who told me that they were progressing with the interior renovation and the new entrance canopy was completely framed, however, they were not in alignment as shown on the drawings. Suddenly, our whole conversation turned into an Abbot and Costello skit. Me: What? Yes, it is centered. Superintendent: No, it isn't. Me: Sure it is! I'm looking at the drawings. Superintendent: I'm looking through a hole in the wall, and they are not centered. We went back and forth for a few minutes questioning what we were both looking at when we started to check some dimensions. We discovered that the dimension locating the exterior entrance canopy was incorrect: the drawing showed the entrance canopy in the correct location, centered on the circular information desk, however the dimension was wrong. Confirmed, the entrance canopy was constructed a few feet off-center of the information desk. Yikes, I thought. Now what?

I had never had anything like this happen on any of my projects before. How would I handle this? I started writing a story in my head. It went something like this: I call the client to see if we can work with what is in place, then they say, no, the canopy must move. I tell my boss about the error and that the canopy has to move; boss turns red with fury, shouts, shouts more and louder, and finally shouts, "You're fired!" This was the story in my head. Talk about a bad ending!

With iterations of the story still swirling around in my head, my heart pounding, and a sense of numbness in my legs,

I started the long walk to my boss's office. Randy sat at his desk looking down at some paperwork. I stood there for a second waiting for him to look up; I did not want to jump right into this career-ending conversation. I finally started telling Randy the issue we'd just discovered, and I hypothesized how this error may have occurred. To my surprise, as the conversation went on, he remained seated and calm—there was no shouting, no sign of anger. We talked about possible solutions. While in his office, we made a call to the client and explained the situation. Sure, the client was upset with the error, but they, too, remained calm and there was no shouting. The client insisted that the canopy had to be centered on the information desk, and that was his final answer.

This meant that the canopy would need to be torn down, piece by piece, and rebuilt, this time in the correct place using the correct dimensions. I stood there ready to wince for what I thought was coming next, termination of my employment. This error was going to cost a lot of money, and someone had to pay with either their money or their job to be held accountable. When we hung up with the client, Randy looked at me and calmly, matter-of-factly, said, "Well, we'll have to move the entrance canopy." Wait for it…wait for it…nothing. No shouting? No, "You're fired" declarations? No, "You'll pay for this!"? Nothing.

Randy objectively looked at the situation, searched for possible solutions rather than assigning blame, took direction from the client, and did what was right by moving the canopy without objection. Randy took the heat from the client for his teammate—me. He showed me compassion and empathy. I am certain he could sense my nervousness and disappointment for the error I had made. He knew that shouting would not solve the problem. We were both in this together, and we were going to solve this issue together. I left his office with my dignity and self-esteem intact, invigorated that we were going to correct the error *together* and move on. This was our problem to solve, not just my problem to solve. We were a team and in it together! It was a great feeling.

The impact this moment left on me was deeper than a meteor crater. It left an indelible mark, an imprint, on who I was and was to be. It changed how I, the future me, would treat others when they made similar errors, and those errors were certain to occur. Randy taught me that the story in your head is just that, your story, the thing you think might happen but also is likely not to, and sometimes that story can be paralyzing. He helped me understand that the story written in your head may be the worst-case scenario. And it's ok to have that story in your head; stoics live by imagining worst-case scenarios because it enables them to accept anything in between and including it. It helps you better prepare for any potential outcome, but you don't have to panic believing it will absolutely come true. Ninety-or-more percent of the time, the answer to what will happen lies somewhere in between.

If Randy would have played out exactly like the story in my head, I may not have had a successful career as an architect. I may not have been able to have a positive impact on my future teammates, and I may not have written this book. This was a drop in the pond that left a positive impact on my landscape and deeply affected my leadership skills.

Regrets

As Frank Sinatra first sang, "Regrets, I've had a few. But then again, too few to mention." I guess I have had a few more than that, so I will mention a few.

Yes, I have behaved poorly. Regrets come in two forms the things we wished we'd have done and things we wish we hadn't. People sometimes ask what regrets you have in life. I view this as a question: what should I have done differently to be more successful?

Working in an office with cubicles, you get to sit feet away from others. The open office is great for seeing and hearing others, but terrible when you need peace and quiet to focus and get stuff done. I would consider myself even-tempered, and I believe those who know me would agree.

Back in the pre-pandemic day, when we were all working in the office, I sat in an area with ten very close workstations and low partitions between them. There was one person I will refer to as "The Whistler." Throughout the day, the whistler would randomly make a whistling sound. A phone rang—the whistle. A cough—the whistle. A loud laugh—then, the whistle. Some people whistle a happy tune, but this was a bit more annoying, like fingernails on a chalkboard.

One day, I approached the whistler and mentioned how distracting his un-merry tune was and if there was something he could do to stop it or if I could help in some way. We talked about some kind of secret sign I could give, a look or something. He agreed he would work on minimizing or eliminating the whistle. Unfortunately, he could not control his puckered whistling. This distracting and now irritating whistle kept floating in the air and making its way to my ears.

On another day, after our discussion, there it was again, that annoying whistle. I do not recall the circumstances preceding it, but I had had it with the whistling! I snapped! I lost control! Like Ralphie stringing together a line of profanity while simultaneously slugging Scut Farkus, I verbally assaulted the whistler in front of my fellow workers. It was out—I cursed him, and I could not take it back. The moment the words left my mouth, I knew I had done wrong to this person and all my other co-workers. I walked away feeling horrible.

The next day, I did what I should have done right away the previous day. I apologized to the whistler and my fellow coworkers for my actions and for what I had said the day before. I learned a few things from this experience. I learned to have enough humility to apologize for your actions when you do wrong and to not wait to do it. We all make mistakes, and it is best to acknowledge them immediately.

Everyone is different, and we need to be more accepting of others. If you are having an issue with someone, do not wait to address it and don't let it get under your skin. If you feel an outburst coming, walk away to calm down and then approach that person one-on-one. We cannot change others, and we shouldn't try. We should be more accepting of others as they come to us. We should strategize with ourselves how we will interact with other personalities as everyone is different, has different habits, and exhibits unique personality traits—some of which may be a health or psychological issue.

Guardian Angels

Have you ever been or met a guardian angel? It was the last day of August in Milwaukee, and the Milwaukee Brewers were playing the Pittsburgh Pirates at American Family Field (then Miller Park). My son, Bradley, and I were headed to the game.

We walked fifteen minutes to the Brewer game from a city street. I was too cheap to pay for parking in the ballpark parking lot and, besides, an evening walk with your son is priceless!

The street we were on is a six-lane, heavily traveled thoroughfare with sidewalks on both sides—very pedestrian-friendly. We noticed an older gentleman, probably in his late seventies, crossing the street from the other side of the road. He was waiting with us at a crosswalk to cross at the same intersection we intended to cross. The man asked if we were walking to the ballgame; we said yes. The light turned, and the walk sign flashed white. We were on our way with the elderly man close behind.

Now, even though this walk to Miller Park is along a busy street with a sidewalk, there is a portion that deviates a bit off the road to a fenced area alongside some abandoned buildings. It can be a bit sketchy and unsafe when it gets dark. When we got to this darker area of the sidewalk, I slowed my pace and asked the man his name—it was Mike. Mike was from Cincinnati, "the Kentucky side," he clarified. We chatted all the way to the park, telling Mike all the wonderful places he and his wife could visit while in Milwaukee. His wife decided to stay back in the hotel and not go with him to the ballgame. After a walk around the outside of Miller Park to show Mike the grounds, we shook hands and parted ways knowing that we made someone's trip to Miller Park and the City of Milwaukee a little more pleasant. We felt that we had taken him under our wing to provide safe and informative travel.

Bradley and I decided to leave the game at the end of the seventh inning; it was already 10 p.m., a school night, and the

Brewers were leading 5-2. Large expanses of glass windows at Miller Park provide great views of the city from the walk inside the building that surrounds the outfield. Walking around the inside perimeter of Miller Park, Bradley surprisingly shouted, "Mike!" To our amazement, our walking companion, Mike, was on the outside of the ballpark right next to the glass window. Out of the all the almost 34,000 attendees, we spotted Mike again. That's like finding a needle in the proverbial haystack. What are the chances?

Mike was talking to security guards trying to figure out how to get back to where he came from. To get to the path that we took does take a bit of explaining. You must cross several ballpark roads and traverse stairs to get to it. Bradley and I quickly changed course and exited the ballpark wanting to catch up with Mike as, even though we could not hear the conversation, we knew what he was asking. We did catch up with Mike and escorted him back to the path and stayed with him until he was in sight of his car. We had another nice conversation as we escorted Mike back to a Chili's restaurant, where his wife was waiting to pick him up.

This experience again made me stop and think. We are put in places and situations by God, to be His good shepherds, to serve others, to help and guide them. We were Mike's guardian angels that night. We were Mike's Clarence. We were put at that place and time by God to walk with one of his sheep. There was also a lesson here for my son and me: I believe God put Mike in our path to help us recognize when being a friend is needed. It is not easy to walk a path with someone you do not know. The conversation can be as awkward as the cadence of the slower than normal walk. Sometimes we need to adjust our gait to match others, change our conversation to better connect, and sometimes we need to let our guard down to help others feel more secure.

February 2020, we were just starting to learn more about COVID-19. I was flying from Milwaukee to Dallas for a conference. My wife Dawn is a Registered Nurse and was aware of the new virus that seemed to be on a rampage to cover the world. As I was packing and preparing to leave home to get to the airport to catch my flight, she strongly suggested—well, told me—to take hand sanitizer and bleach wipes.

She gave instructions that once on the plane, I should wipe down my seat, armrests, and tray table with bleach wipes. She even suggested I take and wear a face mask, just in case. A face mask? That's just crazy talk. If I did that, I would get stared at like I had a third eye. But I, like a good husband, took all the personal protection equipment suggested, just not the face mask. I put it all in my backpack and agreed to do as I was told, mostly. Of course, like a normal husband, once on the plane, my PPE stayed in my backpack.

This was not a direct flight. I would have a short layover in Kansas City. I was in the middle seat with a man on my left and woman on my right, who had the window seat. Once at cruising altitude, I noticed that the woman was sniffing and wiping her nose, a lot. Oh, God, I'm sitting next to a COVID-19 carrier! I thought. I immediately heard my wife's voice shouting in my head, "Wipe down your seat, arm rest…"

As the flight continued and the woman kept sniffing and wiping her nose, I contemplated offering her a few Kleenexes from my backpack. This might help contain the virus I was now assuredly going to get. Would she take my gesture as rude and insensitive? After about fifteen minutes, I took a chance. I pulled out the Kleenex, placed them on her open tray table, and asked if she needed a tissue. She thanked me but did not take them.

A few minutes went by and, to my shock and surprise, she started to talk to me. She told me her story while still wiping her nose. Her father had passed away. She was going home to Kansas City to close the sale of her father's house which she had been cleaning out for the past few months as she traveled back and forth from her home in the Chicago area. Her father had passed away at the beginning of the year and she was having a hard time closing the final chapter of his life and a part of hers. I sat and listened and tried to say things that might give her some comfort—mostly, I sat and let her talk. What could I say? We had just met, and I didn't know her. Her crying subsided and she seemed to relax more as she shared her story; I listened and said very little. I shared some encouraging words and told her that what she was doing was the right thing. We talked all the way to Kansas City, and when we finally parted ways, she seemed to be at peace with what needed to be done.

I believe I was put on that flight by God to help this woman during her time of need. God put me in that place, at that time, to be His ear to this woman. To provide comfort to one of his sheep. I believe that God sometimes puts us in places to help do his work. This was one of those moments that I recognized I needed to act, not respond in fear. I wonder how many of these moments we miss because we are not willing, or quiet enough, ourselves, to listen? I was this woman's Clarence.

While these experiences are not right out of a project management textbook, they taught this project manager and human a few things. Take a chance and reach out when it seems the whole group, or the whole world, is afraid. Always show compassion and empathy for others. Sometimes, just being there for someone is all that is needed, and maybe a hug. I invite you to take a chance, professionally and personally, and be the light of God you are meant to be in all situations. Let God work through you. God can, and frequently does, work through all of us.

WHO YOU ARE IS ENOUGH

So, I'll ask you again, who are you? How did you become who you are, and how will you affect others in a positive way? What shoreline will you affect by the ripple you create when you drop in?

As we set out on this journey of discovery together, I have asked these questions of you. It doesn't matter the field of work you are in; the stories shared here can be applied to all kinds of work and life situations. Look at your own life experiences, the ones that helped hone you. In what ways can you improve yourself by leveraging those experiences?

I hope you do take time to create a career or life plan if you do not have one. Having a plan is important—remember, if you fail to plan you plan to fail. Identify your life's mission, your vision, your beliefs and values.

I hope you have internalized this book and these life experiences to your benefit; to help you to become the person you want to be and enhance your self-esteem, confidence, and leadership skills. But maybe, even more important than helping you, I hope the extension of this book's worth is to assist you in helping others to become who they want to and can become, to boost their self-esteem, confidence, and leadership abilities. If I must resign myself to one definition, that's what being a 3PM Leader is all about.

I am grateful to all those whose lessons helped me in life who are mentioned in this book, and to those who remain unnamed, for it is through each of them that I, like the song from the Broadway hit *Wicked* melodically attests, "have been changed for the better." Remember those in your life who, throughout a lifetime or a fleeting moment, have changed you for the better. Then be one who passes those life experiences positively on to others and changes them for the better.

Finally, I am grateful for life's challenges that have taken me to the brink and required me to dig deep and discover what I am truly made of. For each challenge that changed me for the better, each person who showed me the way to do or NOT to do something, I am grateful. Always be grateful and always be you!

ACKNOWLEDGMENTS

I want to thank those whose drops in my pond helped me successfully write and publish this book.

As I mentioned in this narrative, when I stepped away from my career as an architect, Megan Kocchi, a former colleague of mine sent me a note and told me that my newfound time on my hands would allow me to write the book I had always talked about. Megan, if it wasn't for this thoughtful reminder, this book may not have come to fruition. Thank you.

To Laurie and Mark Kallas for allowing me to spend time thinking, reflecting and writing in the serenity of their isolated river-banked property, and to my sister, Cathy, and my brother-in-law, Scott, for presenting the idea to ask Laurie and Mark to "use their property"—thank you!

Writing a book and being an independent publisher takes a team. I was able to assemble a great team with the help of Susie Schaefer from Finish the Book Publishing, LLC, who guided my every step (and believe me, there were plenty of them!) To my editor, Lisa Shrewsberry for taking my manuscript and polishing it into a real gem—my sincere thanks.

To all my colleagues who shaped me through my failings and successes—thank you! Each one of you gave me something that made me better at what I did. Everyone says you won't miss the job when you leave a career, it's the people that you'll miss, and this is certainly true. I think of my colleagues fondly and often.

To my Grandpa William Mauritz, who has been gone for many years but still echoes in my head, for instilling in me a can-do attitude with the worse outcome being someone saying "no"—thank you.

To my children Bradley and Kaytlyn: Through your eyes I was able to see what was important. You showed me how to be compassionate, humble, helpful, and caring. Thanks for taking me along for the ride... but that's another story!

To my wife, Dawn, for allowing me the time to be away physically and mentally while writing. You have supported me in my journey of walking away from a great career and supporting me to discover my "what's next." It takes courage to step into the unknown, and I am forever thankful you stepped with both feet into this new journey with me.

I was fearless and took a road less traveled, for me never traveled, and authored this book to give others a path to follow, a glimpse into how one's life can be affected by others. I hope that the words you read, the feelings you felt, will be a drop to change your shoreline for the better. Even more importantly, I hope you see how you can enhance others' self-esteem, confidence, and leadership through your actions.

ABOUT THE AUTHOR

Early in life, Bob recognized how humans are interconnected and how much power each possesses to affect another. He noticed how one could easily disappoint, sadden, or humiliate, but also how one could uplift, enlighten, and encourage.

Bob was born in a small town in the middle of Wisconsin. His family espoused Midwest values and influences, and included his father, a firefighter, his stay-at-home mom, and two sisters. He was the storied middle child. Although born within the GenX generation, he more closely aligned with baby boomer values and characteristics. His creative flare included an interest in photography, drawing, building, and aviation. With Oshkosh being the mecca of flight, Bob was exposed to airplanes from a young age. Several high school friends became pilots and, later in life when his son sought his own pilot's license, Bob also began flight instruction. Bob received his sport pilot certificate in 2010 and has flown well over 500 hours.

Prior to graduating high school, Bob's career interests led him to explore the military and law enforcement, however, he became the first in his family to attend a university, encouraged by his future wife, Dawn, to pursue a career in architecture. Bob spent most of the 1990s and 2000s creating a home and family with Dawn that has since expanded with grandchildren and deep, caring friendships.

Bob has worked as a licensed architect since 1992, completing building projects in many market sectors including education, healthcare, retail, industrial, residential, and hospitality. He spent the last twenty-five years of his career focused on learning environments, making it his personal mission to rethink school design and construction.

Throughout Bob's career, he had the opportunity to lead project teams, become a principal and shareholder at a leading architectural firm, and support the Learning Environments Studio as its director, leading a staff of thirty-five-plus people spanning several office locations. Here, he advanced design by challenging his team and his clients to be innovative and futuristic. His greatest reward is seeing others enjoy and flourish in the spaces he helped bring to fruition.

Bob is an Accredited Learning Environment Planner (ALEP) through the Association for Learning Environments (A4LE). He has attained the level of Construction Document Technologist (CDT) through the Construction Specifications Institute (CSI) certification program. He has also attained LEED AP through the USGBC LEED accreditation process.

An avid runner, Bob also has hundreds of miles to his credit and has completed two half-marathons.

Becoming an author was not something Bob set as an early goal, however, as he has often told his children and others, "You can do anything and be anybody if you set your mind to it. All it takes is setting a goal, expending effort, and never giving up!"

Bob continues living that mantra and accomplishing more than he would ever have imagined. He firmly believes in the words of the great Jedi Master Yoda– "Do or do not. There is no try."

SOURCES & RESOURCES

Covey, S. R. (1997). *The Seven Habits of Highly Effective People: Restoring the Character Ethic.* Macmillan Reference USA.

Gross, C. (2010, November 30). *The stages of a flower from seed to bloom.* Hunker. https://www.hunker.com/13426298/the-stages-of-a-flower-from-seed-to-bloom/

Hazardous Attitudes; *Activities, courses, seminars & Webinars-ALC_Content-FAA-FAASTeam-FAASafety.gov.* (n.d.). https://www.faasafety.gov/gslac/ALC/course_content.aspx?cID=723&sID=1448&preview=true

Pilot's Handbook of Aeronautical Knowledge. 2016. Chapter 2, pp. 2-5. *What is the DiSC assessment?* (n.d.). Discprofile.com. https://www.discprofile.com/what-is-disc

Barb Bickford – bickfordcollaboration.com/about

Climer Cards – https://climercards.com

Sandy Salvo – centered-connections.com

LETTERS
TO THE
GRIEVING

Moving Through Loss and
Disappointment to Healing and Hope

KATIE LUSE

Edited by Susan Thompson
Cover Design by Kristen Ingebretson
Proofread by Jennifer Cullis, Printopyia LLC
Interior Design by A. Banales, Printopya LLC
Headshot Photo by Natalie Zigarovich

Published by Luse Productions, LLC
www.katieluse.com

Paperback ISBN: 979-8-9864243-3-0
eISBN: 979-8-9864243-4-7

First Edition (Re-Titled from *Lampposts: Letters To The Grieving*)

Printed in the United States.